MW00992388

Conflict and Resolution

Second Edition

ASPEN PUBLISHERS

Conflict and Resolution

Second Edition

Barbara A. Nagle Lechman
Associate Professor
Montclair State University

Wolters Kluwer
Law & Business

.USTIN   BOSTON   CHICAGO   NEW YORK   THE NETHERLANDS

Aspen Publishers
Attn: Permissions Department
76 Ninth Avenue, 7th Floor
New York, NY 10011-5201

To contact Customer Care, e-mail customer.care@aspenpublishers.com, call 1-800-234-1660, fax 1-800-901-9075, or mail correspondence to:

Aspen Publishers
Attn: Order Department
PO Box 990
Frederick, MD 21705

Printed in the United States of America.

4 5 6 7 8 9 0

ISBN 978-0-7355-6732-0

Library of Congress Cataloging-in-Publication Data

Nagle-Lechman, Barbara A., 1944–
    Conflict and resolution / Barbara A. Nagle-Lechman. — 2nd ed.
        p. cm.
    Includes bibliographical references and index.
    ISBN 978-0-7355-6732-0
    1. Dispute resolution (Law) — United States. 2. Arbitration and award — United States.
3. Mediation — United States. 4 Negotiation. 5. Conflict management. I. Title.

KF9084.N35 2008
347.73'9–dc22   2007038177

About Wolters Kluwer Law & Business

Wolters Kluwer Law & Business is a leading provider of research information and work-flow solutions in key specialty areas. The strengths of the individual brands of Aspen Publishers, CCH, Kluwer Law International and Loislaw are aligned within Wolters Kluwer Law & Business to provide comprehensive, in-depth solutions and expert-authored content for the legal, professional and education markets.

CCH was founded in 1913 and has served more than four generations of business professionals and their clients. The CCH products in the Wolters Kluwer Law & Business group are highly regarded electronic and print resources for legal, securities, antitrust and trade regulation, government contracting, banking, pension, payroll, employment and labor, and healthcare reimbursement and compliance professionals.

Aspen Publishers is a leading information provider for attorneys, business professionals and law students. Written by preeminent authorities, Aspen products offer analytical and practical information in a range of specialty practice areas from securities law and intellectual property to mergers and acquisitions and pension/benefits. Aspen's trusted legal education resources provide professors and students with high-quality, up-to-date and effective resources for successful instruction and study in all areas of the law.

Kluwer Law International supplies the global business community with comprehensive English-language international legal information. Legal practitioners, corporate counsel and business executives around the world rely on the Kluwer Law International journals, loose-leafs, books and electronic products for authoritative information in many areas of international legal practice.

Loislaw is a premier provider of digitized legal content to small law firm practitioners of various specializations. Loislaw provides attorneys with the ability to quickly and efficiently find the necessary legal information they need, when and where they need it, by facilitating access to primary law as well as state-specific law, records, forms and treatises.

Wolters Kluwer Law & Business, a unit of Wolters Kluwer, is headquartered in New York and Riverwoods, Illinois. Wolters Kluwer is a leading multinational publisher and information services company.

Summary of Contents

Table of Contents

Preface

The goal of this book is to provide students with an understanding of conflict and a working knowledge of the three major forms of dispute resolution—negotiation, mediation, and arbitration. It is my hope that students will apply the theory and practice of dispute resolution to their personal as well as their professional lives.

The first two chapters concern the nature and diverse sources of conflict, and offer an overview of conflict resolution processes. Then, in chapters 3-5, more careful consideration is given to negotiation, mediation, and arbitration, respectively. The last two chapters serve as an introduction to other forms of dispute resolution in the legal context and to selected policy and ethical issues in the field. Each chapter concludes with a summary and exercises designed to engage students in knowledge application, integration, and expansion. Some chapters include role plays to allow students to experience how the theories of dispute resolution are practiced. The confidential information for each role play, plus additional role plays, can be found in the Instructor's Manual.

There are a number of ways this book can be used. It has served as the basic text in an undergraduate course. It could also be used in a section of a course. Finally, it could be the basis of a unit on dispute resolution in a course of study.

This new edition brings some international references, reflecting a greater appreciation for our global existence as well as my broadening international experience. Since writing the first edition, I have had the benefit of teaching in Nepal and presenting in Spain. I have also participated in the United State Institute of Peace's faculty seminar on international conflict resolution, thereby accessing a wonderful resource and learning a great deal more about international conflict and peace making.

There are more web references in this edition, based on an ever-increasing web presence in our lives. My students engage in online real time negotiation and mediation role plays. I plan on expanding my online experience to Second Life and applying that to my students' learning experience. I urge students and faculty alike to continue exploring both web resources and the tools of technology in conflict management.

We as mediators and educators have seen the discipline of mediation expand since the first edition, with the emergence of new models, greater application of mediation in various disciplines, and more research available to students. That expanded knowledge base permeates Chapter 4.

The second edition includes further changes and additions arising from continuous learning, practicing, reflection, and teaching in the full field of Conflict and Conflict Resolution. The literature has greatly expanded, and Codes of Conduct and ethical guidelines have changed. Some role plays have been modified based on classroom experience, and others have been added to enhance the students' active learning experience.

I would like to thank my colleagues and teachers at the Hewlitt Institute for Socio-Legal Dispute Resolution at The Ohio State University in 1993, several of whom read preliminary drafts: Carol King, Tom Grexa, and Theresa Hagen. I would also like to thank friends and colleagues closer to home who have looked at drafts and made suggestions: Joseph Ryan, Rosalie Cannone McGill, Sheila O'Shea Criscione, and Marilyn Tayler. My students at Montclair State University have been a great source of inspiration and continue to teach me and improve my teaching in this field. My graduate assistant, Rich Adams, and several students who worked with me at various stages in the process, including Viki Giammarella and Dina Sadik, all contributed to the final product. The individual who contributed the most to the production of this book is a former student and now a colleague, attorney and adjunct professor Louis A. Chiafullo. Finally, I want to thank my husband, George Lechman, who always helps me experience conflict and its resolution from a very personal perspective and who provides ongoing support in so many ways that make life beautiful.

In connection with this revised edition, I would like to thank Quatey Franklin, a graduate student who assisted with research, Rhiannon Cunnah, a student who did some proofreading, and faculty who used the text and gave valuable input, including Joanne Bochis, Sheila Criscione, Paula Eisen, Cort Engelken, and Tom Zeringo, as well as Auram Segall for his contribution of several new role plays. On a personal level, I want to again thank my dear husband, George Lechman, for his *daily* support and my friend Winsome Tennant for her friendship and prayer.

Barbara Nagle Lechman

September 2007

Acknowledgments

The author gratefully acknowledges the permissions granted to reproduce the following materials:

Code of Ethics for Arbitrators in Commercial Disputes (2004). American Arbitration Association and American Bar Association. Reprinted with permission.

Conflict Between People and Groups, Causes, Processes, and Resolutions 1st edition by WORCHEL/SIMPSON 1993. Reprinted with permission of Wadsworth, a division of Thomson Learning: www.thomsonrights.com. Fax 800 730 2215.

Goldberg, Stephen B., Sander, Frank E. A., & Rogers, Nancy H., Cole, Sarah Rudolph *Dispute Resolution: Negotiation, Mediation, and Other Processes* (5th ed. 2007). Copyright © 2007 by Aspen Publishers. Reprinted with permission.

Mclver, John P. & Keilitz, Susan, Court-Annexed Arbitration: An Introduction, 14 Justice Systems Journal, No. 2, Copyright ©1991 National Center for State Courts. Used with Permission.

Model Standards of Conduct for Mediators (2005). American Arbitration Association, American Bar Association, and Association for Conflict Resolution. Reprinted with permission. Reproduced with permission from the Association for Conflict Resolution (ACR), www.ACRnet.org

Reprinted by Permission of the publisher from The Art and Science of Negotiation: How to Resolve Conflicts and Get the Best Out of Bargaining by Howard Raiffa, 11-19, 47, 54, 78, 102, 110-111, 142-144, 148, 198, 205-217, 218, 220, 252, 254, 346, Cambridge, Mass.: The Belknap Press of Harvard University Press, Copyright ©1982 by the President and Fellows of Harvard College.

Reprinted from *Ending It: Dispute Resolution in America: Descriptions, Examples Cases, and Questions* with permission. Copyright 1990 Matthew Bender & Company, Inc., a member of the LexisNexis Group. All rights reserved.

Sander, Frank E. A., The Courthouse and Alternative Dispute Resolution, reprinted in *Negotiation Strategies for Mutual Gain: The Basic Seminar of the Program on Negotiation at Harvard Law School* (Lavinia Hall, ed. 1993). SAGE Publications, Inc., Newbury Park. Reprinted with permission.

Scott, Gini Graham, PhD.*Disagreements, Disputes, and All Out War* by AMACOM. (2007). *www.ginigrahamscott.com* and *www.workingwithhumans.com*.

Singer, Linda R., *Settling Disputes: Conflict Resolution in Business, Families, and The Legal System* (2d ed. 1994). Copyright © 1994 by West-view Press. Reprinted by permission of The Perseus Book Group.

Yarn, Douglas H., ed., *Dictionary of Conflict Resolution* (1999). Reprinted with permission of John Wiley & Sons, Inc.

Conflict and Resolution

Second Edition

Introduction

1

Jennifer Rose and Charles Finnery have been partners in the practice of law for eight years. In the beginning it appeared that their talents complemented one another. Jennifer was the litigator and the person who brought in most of the business. Charles took care of the office management and did residential real estate, trusts and estates work, and some small corporate work. They never entered into a formal partnership agreement because they were friends before they started the partnership. For the past five years, you have worked as their paralegal and really enjoy the variety of work, the relaxed way they run their office, and the flexible working schedule they permit you to follow.

For the last six months, however, things have been tense in the office and are getting increasingly worse. You don't know the source of the problem, but both Charles and Jennifer are miserable and it is rubbing off on you. Sometimes they explode into shouting matches and name-calling, which you find very unprofessional. You know from doing the bookkeeping that income is down and you think it may be due to the present situation. Things have gotten so bad that you have considered quitting. Even if you stay, the partnership may break up and neither attorney could afford you on their own. The truth is you like Jennifer and Charles a great deal and it saddens you to see what is happening. . . . It's almost like a divorce!

Can you suggest anything to help Jennifer and Charles through their present struggle? You don't want to get caught in the middle, but you do want things to return to the way they were before this conflict started. What can you do?

Or, consider another scenario: you and your family live in a small town in a southwestern state. There is a significant amount of agriculture and your family owns a feed store that is frequented by the local farmers. Quite a number of years ago, the farm owners began bringing in labor from another country, because the people worked hard and did not require as much pay as some of the local laborers. The workers were originally migrant, following the plantings and harvests around the countryside. However, within the last couple of years, they have begun to stay and put down roots. You know that some of them are undocumented immigrants, but some of them are legal. The local economy has come to depend on them, not only for the labor they provide, but for their spending in local places of business. Their children attend the local school and they are trying to integrate into community life.

However, a number of community people are "up in arms" over the influx of these foreigners and do not want them to stay in their community. They are trying to influence the town "fathers" to do something to get rid of the immigrants, regardless of their legal status. The foreigners do not speak English well, do not follow the same customs as the local people, and are "changing the character" of the town.

You are selling off a small portion of your land and one of the foreigners wants to purchase it. You are very concerned about how the original people in the town will react if you sell your property to this outsider, who, by the way, is legally in the country. However, no one else has expressed an interest in buying your property, and the realtor tells you that by law you cannot discriminate against someone who is financially able to buy your property.

You don't feel strongly either way about the foreigners, but don't want to be caught in this conflict. What you do may affect the family business. The town has become polarized over this issue. What can you do? Where can you seek help? It seems like no matter what you do, you will lose.

Introductory Notes

This book explores conflicts like the foregoing as well as a variety of others; it considers how they develop, how they affect the parties in conflict as well as society at large, and how conflict resolution processes[1] and our legal system respond to them. The goal is to enable readers to understand and accept conflict in their own lives, in their communities, in the legal environment, and in the *larger global context*. Then, the readers are introduced to a number of conflict resolution theories and techniques so that they can understand and, in some cases, be able to apply those techniques. The final goal is to enable individuals to understand and be prepared to participate in the processes in which conflicts and disputes are managed and resolved.

This book is written for undergraduate and graduate students who are interested in the nature of conflict and its resolution. The reader should bear in mind that there are diverse approaches to this subject. Alternate dispute resolution (ADR) is very much a part of the landscape today, and it is imperative that everyone be familiar with the ADR processes available to them.

The model and language of conflict and its resolution that is developed here is the one that permeates the dominant culture in the United States. This has been called the "European Model." While a consideration of other techniques and systems is beyond the scope of this book, one needs to be aware that there are other conflict resolution models both in the United States and throughout the world that justify further study. For example, the neutrality of the third party is seen as very important in the United States. However, in some countries, and in some settings, the parties would not want a "neutral" third party, but rather someone who has an interest in resolving the conflict. Cultural differences also influence conflict, perceptions of conflict, and conflict resolution.

---

1 Throughout the court system, these processes are frequently referred to as *alternate dispute resolution* (ADR). In some jurisdictions, such as New Jersey, they are called *complementary dispute resolution*. They are often simply referred to as *dispute resolution*.

Perceptions of conflict and its role can vary in different cultures. For example, conflict must remain private in some Eastern cultures and to expose it to an outsider or to public scrutiny by taking it to court can be a terrible embarrassment. In a collectivist culture, harmony is more important than individual differences and the community may have a process for addressing conflict that is relatively unfamiliar to westerners, such as talking circles.

Conflict's Impact and the Necessity of Understanding Conflict

Conflict Is Pervasive

Individuals and groups are faced with conflict from the beginning of life to its end. A baby cries because it wants something, but the baby's parents do not always know what the infant wants. This conflict arises from the inability to communicate effectively. A child wants to play with her friends instead of doing homework. There is a conflict between the child and her parent as a result of differing values. A young adult wishes to continue her education beyond an undergraduate degree and seeks parental support. While the parents may want to help their daughter, financial constraints prohibit it. An adult may want to enter into a second marriage against the wishes of the children. Conflict arises in employment situations regarding salary, working conditions, personnel, and related issues. (The opening scenario at the beginning of this chapter is an example of work-related conflict that extends beyond salary). An elderly person may wish to continue to live independently, while the children fear for his safety and security if such independent living continues. Purchasers and sellers of houses, autos, and other significant items frequently disagree on the value of such items.

A group of individuals — bound together by the commitment to common values — may clash with other groups espousing different values over such issues as abortion, free speech, entitlements, and gun control. It sometimes appears that, as a nation, we are divided among political, racial, ethnic, gender, class, economic, and creedal lines.

Companies and similar organizations are also conflicted. They enter into contracts that may result in an unsatisfactory relationship, creating a dispute between the parties to the contract. There may be conflicts between subdivisions of an organization resulting from a disagreement over territory or resources, such as departments within a school vying for limited funds. There are conflicts within organizations over management policies. Conflicts also arise when employees or groups of employees believe they should receive greater compensation or more extensive benefits and the employer does not agree.

Conflict resolution and alternative dispute resolution are exemplified in labor management relations. Labor union agreements have traditionally included hearings, arbitration, or mediation as a system for dispute resolution. Employer/employee conflicts in the private sector are resolved through grievance procedures and ADR processes governed largely by labor union contracts. While the early part of this century saw the rise of private sector labor contracts, the latter part of this century has shown a significant decline of unionization in the private sector with the growth of unionization in the public sector. However, both the means to reach agreement as well as the application of agreements continue to require the dispute resolution methods considered here.

Government, in all of its manifestations, is also faced with daily conflict. Elections are a result, at least in part, of conflicting ideas. The scenario at the beginning of the chapter demonstrates a community conflict which reflects a conflict over national policy. Different branches of government have different agendas, giving rise to adverse interests. State and county governments may disagree on which of them is financially responsible for the court system. A shortage of resources can contribute to such disputes. A nation may be conflicted over various domestic and foreign policies, planned or implemented. Nations find themselves faced with seemingly insurmountable disputes both within their borders and with other nations. In some regions of the world, conflicts span generations and appear intractable.

In the United States, we are very litigious. This means, among other things, that we take many of our conflicts to courts of law for resolution. While a vast majority of lawsuits are settled out of court prior to trial, the reason a plaintiff brings a lawsuit is to seek the court's intervention and ultimate rendering of a decision regarding the dispute.

Reaction to Conflict

It is clear that conflict cannot be avoided. In fact, conflict probably should not be avoided entirely. It can have beneficial results and be viewed as an opportunity for enhanced communication and positive change. It can range from destructive to constructive, for one or all parties, and in both its existence and resolution. Conflict needs to be recognized, understood, and managed or resolved.

A list of conflicts and potential conflicts can be endless, and people in the United States tend to deal with conflicts in a variety of ways. The first, at one end of the continuum, is conflict *avoidance*. People may avoid conflict for a variety of reasons, including their fear of its effect on a relationship, or their general discomfort with conflict. While some might believe this to be a laudatory goal, it is probably not possible for any individual to achieve and it may not be psychologically healthy. Similarly, avoidance is not an appropriate business practice for a company.

If a school district that has used one vendor for a particular service for the last ten years suddenly stops calling the vendor for that service, the vendor could ignore the slight and probably not keep the school district as a client. Alternatively, the vendor could contact the school district and inquire as to why it stopped calling for the service and perhaps discover that there was a misunderstanding, miscommunication, or a fee arrangement that could be set right through negotiation with the district. The result of confronting the conflict would then be a continued, mutually satisfactory business relationship.

The next technique to note along the continuum is *accommodation*. Here, one party gives in to the wishes or demands of the other party, either because they really want to avoid the conflict but the other party wishes to address it, or because "winning" this particular conflict is not that important to them. Like avoidance, this approach can have both positive and negative outcomes. Accommodation can be part of a relationship, so long as the parties "take turns" accommodating. For example, colleagues may alternate who chooses where they go for lunch. On the negative side, if one party always accommodates the other, the relationship is unequal and the accommodator will ultimately resent the other.

Compromise occurs when each party "gives up something to get something." A common example of compromise is demonstrated by a negotiation over the price of an article. Each party moves either up or down from his or her original position until they reach a price that is mutually acceptable. Many people were taught that this is the "fair" way to resolve conflicts. The benefit is that all parties get something that they want. However, not all conflicts are amenable to compromise — some issues cannot be compromised, or there may be a better way of addressing the conflict.

Collaboration has been identified as the "win/win" approach. The parties work together to share their interests and create solutions that meet those interests. For example, an employee asks for a raise, but the employer is unwilling or unable to give the raise. If they collaborate, the employee may share her concern that her job title does not reflect the work she is doing, or that she has been working long hours and not been paid for overtime. The employer may share its inability to raise salary at this time, but could offer a review at a designated time in the future, a new job title that reflects the work being done, or encourage the employee to limit her hours to the ones she is being paid for. For an extensive treatment of this approach, see Roger Fisher and Bill Ury's *Getting to Yes*.

Finally, *confrontation/competition* describes the approach wherein the parties address the conflict directly and each vies to get the most for himself or herself. Like the approaches to conflict listed above, this approach can be seen as negative and positive. An example of a negative result could be a damaged relationship between the parties because of competitive win/lose reasoning. On the other hand, if the parties are able to resolve their conflict by addressing it directly and each competing for what he/she wants, they may resolve the conflict and focus their energy elsewhere. Sometimes, confrontation can turn violent. One reason for the interference of the courts in the lives of individuals is to provide a solution to conflict that avoids violence.

For a more thorough treatment of conflict resolution styles, see Thomas-Kilman Conflict Mode Instrument (TKI), published by CPP, Inc. (formerly Consulting Psychologists Press), *http://www.cpp.com/products/index.asp*. It should also be borne in mind that people use different conflict modes depending on where and with whom the conflict takes place. People respond differently to conflict at home and conflict at work, for example.

A person's reaction to conflict will vary with the type of conflict faced, such as a professional disagreement versus a gang war, as well as the skills each individual has developed to deal with conflict. Conflict seldom occurs in a vacuum, or in private. Frequently there is an audience that has an impact on how the parties respond to each other and what conflict approaches they utilize. Audiences rally on both sides of the conflict, expressing their opinions, encouraging certain actions, and altering the balance of power. A positive example of using the power of an audience can be found in Mahatma Ghandi's and Martin Luther King Jr.'s abilities to bring their non-violent resistance to the attention of the world, thereby raising moral support for their cause.

Once a conflict develops into a dispute recognizable as one for which our judicial system may provide a remedy, there can be another whole series of dispute resolution methods. The most recognized is "taking him to court," also known as "I'll see you in court." Before the conflicting parties make it to court, however, they sometimes choose or are directed to participate in one of the dispute resolution processes that are the subject of this book. The movement encouraging the use of these processes has a number of sources and rationales, including an expansion of individual rights, the time and emotional costs of litigation, and the effort to empower people to participate in the resolution of their own disputes.

No one resolution method is the answer to all conflicts. There is no panacea. However, each method or some combination of them may play a necessary role in each dispute. Their use may be further dictated by considerations of time, resources, relational impact, nature of the parties, and the nature of the conflict.

Sources of Conflict

While it is tempting to lay responsibility for conflict at the feet of one significant instigator, it is clear that conflict arises in a variety of situations, in distinctive configurations, and from different sources. It is likely that one's background and experience, the "lenses" through which one views the world, will influence one's perception as to the real source of conflict. Readers may find some overlap in the following discussion regarding sources of conflict and may disagree. The point is that the source of conflict must be critically examined before a responsive strategy can be developed.

A major source of misunderstandings that lead to conflict is communication breakdown due to ineffective communication patterns. If parties cannot communicate, or do not understand one another, it is unlikely that they will be able to resolve differences or "work out their problems." An indicator of the pervasiveness of this problem is that mediation training invariably directs neutrals to aid the parties in improving their ability to communicate with one another.

Another significant contributor to conflict is a power imbalance between the parties, which is taken advantage of by the more powerful one. If one of the parties is more powerful, she is in a position to require the other to comply with her will. This more powerful party may be an individual, an organization, or a country. Such an exercise of power will likely anger and frustrate the less powerful party, and the more powerful disputant will lose respect for the weaker one. Additionally, the blatant exercise of power by one party over the other can leave the weaker party waiting for the next opportunity to even the score. Again, the mediation literature speaks of the need to be sensitive to the balance of power between disputing parties.

Power shifts during a relationship are similarly causative. For example, if a husband had previously been the major provider of the family income and decides, or is forced, to stay home and care for the family because the wife lands a better job, power within the family may shift and cause relational difficulty. Similarly, in the work environment, if a professional is promoted and made supervisor of her previous peers, power has shifted and will likely cause conflict. In many conflicts within nations, when one party, religious, or ethnic group is in power, it abuses members of the other party, religion, or ethnic group. Thereafter, the second party comes into power and abuses members of the first party, and the cycle continues. There have been examples of this in many areas of the world, including Ireland, Indonesia, Rwanda, and Bosnia and Herzegovina, to name a few.

Economics influence conflict in various ways. If the parties have different economic resources, it can create a power imbalance. If there are insufficient resources, parties will fight over the limited resources available. Biases are sometimes built upon economic differences and may result in a perception of differing values. One party may be jealous of another's financial success, resulting in friction between them. If employees with the same title and job responsibilities are paid differing salaries, even though they have similar experience levels, conflict will result.

Divergent values between individuals, organizations and groups, and nations and cultures can contribute to the disruption of harmony. One must be aware, however, that the claim of differing values is sometimes used to conceal unexpressed pecuniary or emotional interests that may be at the heart of the dispute. Conflicts that do arise from value differences sometimes result in the parties disputing over a "matter of principle." When this happens, attempts to have them reach a satisfactory compromise are difficult. However, if each party understands that the conflict arises from divergent value systems, they may be more empathic toward each other and more able to manage the conflict.

Out of a desire for comfort and similarity, individuals, groups, and sovereigns distance themselves from others whose values they perceive to be different. This can lead to misunderstanding, poor communication, and other conflict instigators. Racial, ethnic, and cultural differences must be considered. However, stereotyping encourages disputants and neutrals to overlook the individual and perceive only generalized attributes. Such behavior is unlikely to contribute to conflict resolution and may actually contribute to the conflict.

Injustice is a significant source of conflict. Think about the civil rights movement in the United States in the 1960s — it was an effort to address injustices brought about by individual and institutional racism. There are examples of injustice from individual to international. If someone is the victim of injustice, she will attempt to access just treatment, and such a demand is seldom met with open arms. Rather, such a demand is resisted, resulting in conflict and sometimes violence.

A less significant but important contributor to conflict is the differing experience levels of the participants. While it is foolish to tout experience as the precursor to wisdom, experience combined with reflection can and should contribute to knowledge and a broader problem-solving resource base. Inexperience, on the other hand, may actually result in a more creative approach. Parties with different levels of experience need to remain open to the other and maintain mutual respect.

Disputants' sensitivity levels can be placed on a continuum, both extremes being factors that contribute to conflict problems. On one end are the insensitive parties. These are people who are totally unconcerned with anyone other than themselves. On the other end are the parties who are overly sensitive and believe that whatever is said is directed at them. Such attributes interfere with productive communication and relationship maintenance.

A dispute or conflict begins on one level but rarely remains there. Conflicts can dissipate or escalate. Escalation occurs, either over the original problem, over the process utilized to resolve it, or due to the insensitivity of one party to the existence of the conflict. Parties personalize communications and become entrenched in their positions. Therefore, students of conflict must be aware of the stage of escalation the conflict has reached to better understand the parties and their dispute.

Another source of conflict is societal change. Historically, religious leaders, precepts of a given faith, respect for the guidance of elders or family members, and social mores were factors that ensured conflict avoidance and resolution. Those who "played by the rules" had a measure of predictability as to the outcome of their actions. With the change of family, religious, and social structure, individuality has replaced conformity and uncertainty has replaced predictability. The world community now observes numerous seemingly intractable conflicts: Israel and Palestine, Sudan, and Sri Lanka, for example. There is a specific area of conflict studies addressing intractable or deep rooted, long-term conflict. Many people are analyzing and developing models for the management of intractable conflict. It would appear that this needs to be one of the focuses of future study.

Finally, what appears to be the immediate or current conflict may just be the top layer. If parties have had previous conflicts, one or both may be angry over a previous wrong, may have suppressed their anger when that wrong occurred, and may now be "getting even." The party may then be less likely to engage in conflict resolution or less likely to trust the other party. Simply resolving the surface problem is unlikely to keep the parties out of future conflicts. Some theories state that the parties need to transform their conflict experience, including how they perceive one another.

This by no means exhausts the list of the origins of conflict; it is meant to lead the reader into considering other sources. There is a more detailed exposition in the next chapter. Understanding the source of a particular conflict can contribute to its effective management and resolution. Frequently, the problem is not what appears on the surface, but another conflict of an ongoing nature which is below the surface and unspoken.

Overview of Conflict Resolution Processes

Negotiation

The form of conflict resolution that most people practice throughout life is negotiation. When one person wants something and another does not want to give it to him, the two people negotiate. The teen who wants certain privileges negotiates with the parent for those privileges. A student who believes she earned a higher grade than the one she received may negotiate with the professor to raise the grade. A legal assistant negotiates with a vendor regarding services provided to the law firm. Non-profit organizations within a community may negotiate with a municipality for their piece of a "block grant." The Pentagon negotiated with state governments regarding the closing of army bases within their states. Nations negotiate issues related to environment and trade — even peace agreements are negotiated.

Black's Law Dictionary (8th. ed. 2004) defines "negotiation" as "[t]he deliberation, discussions, or conference upon the terms of a proposed agreement; the act of settling or arranging the terms and conditions of a bargain, sale, or other business transaction." While the definitions of negotiation in *Dictionary of Conflict Resolution*, edited by Douglas H. Yarn (1999), are thorough and extensive, simply put, negotiation is a "bilateral or multilateral process in which parties who differ over a particular issue attempt to reach agreement or compromise over that issue through communication." In negotiation, a person either represents himself or is represented by an advocate or an agent, frequently over an extended period of time and a number of meetings or communications. Theoretically, the give-and-take process of negotiation between the parties leads to a resolution or agreement that is acceptable to both parties. Sometimes a resolution does not result.

Unlike most of the other forms of conflict resolution, negotiation does not involve the participation of a third-party neutral. It is usually voluntary and participatory. It can occur in a formal or informal setting and can be accomplished in person, by telephone, synchronous or asynchronous communication (such as chat or e-mail), or through written communication. Most people have participated in some form of negotiation, either personal or professional, and have developed some negotiation style of their own.

Mediation

Mediation utilizes the skills of a third-party neutral. A third-party neutral is a person, or sometimes a panel of people, who is not involved in the dispute but participates in the process designed to reach a solution. In the mediation process, the third-party neutral, also known as the mediator, does not determine the outcome of the conflict but rather assists the disputing parties in reaching their own resolution. The mediator is, among other things, a facilitator rather than a judge. Mediation has been called "guided negotiation."

While mediation is less familiar to the layperson than negotiation, examples of it can be found outside the legal process. For instance, conflicted parties sometimes seek the assistance of a religious leader to help them work through their difficulties. In families, a senior member of the family may be sought out for her guidance in settling a conflict. In some homogeneous communities, a well-respected elder may be asked to resolve a dispute within the community. Sometimes these dispute resolutions take the form of arbitration, where the neutral renders a decision settling the matter. At other times, however, the neutral assists the parties in fashioning their own settlement. These are forms of mediation.

There are opportunities for laypeople to serve as mediators, either as volunteers within their community or as compensated professionals. Programs that utilize the abilities of trained mediators can be found across the country. For example, a community-based program will train and supervise citizens to serve as mediators in community disputes. Some college campuses train students or residence assistants in mediation and provide peer mediation to aid in the resolution of conflicts between students. In some states, condominium association bylaws are required to include mediation as an option available to the settlement of disputes between condo owners.

In addition, paralegals in a law firm or governmental agency may prepare cases and witnesses for mediation in the same manner as they prepare cases for trial. Some paralegals are employed in administrative positions in mediation programs. For example, a paralegal may work in a court clerk's office and function as the mediation administrator/supervisor. It is important, therefore, to understand the process and its application. Most importantly, the communication skills that one develops as a result of mediation training contribute to expanded interpersonal competence and can be utilized in many situations.

Attorneys are involved in mediation in several ways. They represent their clients in a mediation process, or they may provide for mediation or other dispute resolution process in a contract they are preparing for a client. They may recommend that a client utilize mediation services, or they may serve as mediators themselves. Some attorneys receive mediation training in law school, while others acquire the skills through private or court-annexed dispute resolution training.

Mediation can take place either privately or under the auspices of the courts. Private mediations are available through private (non-court) organizations such as the American Arbitration Association or a local practicing mediator or group of mediators. When it is under the direction of the court, a judge may refer disputants to a private mediator or may direct parties to participate in mediation at the courthouse. In many jurisdictions, court-annexed mediators must meet minimum educational or training requirements. Non-attorneys are actively involved in mediation as well, and there are few licensing or educational requirements for private mediators, except when they work under the auspices of a particular agency or the court. There are particular areas of mediation practice in which both attorneys and mental health professionals share the arena, i.e., divorce and custody mediation.

Arbitration

Arbitration has a long and distinguished history in certain areas of conflict, e.g., labor and commercial disputes. Arbitration is a conflict resolution process that, like mediation, utilizes the services of a third-party neutral. It is very different, however, from mediation. Arbitration is a more formal process than mediation, in which the arbitrator holds a hearing, listens to testimony and evidence presented by the parties or their attorney, and makes an award. It is similar in nature to a trial, except it is generally held in a more informal environment and is not bound by many of the requirements[2] that a court of law is obliged to follow. Arbitrators may be attorneys, but it is equally likely that an arbitrator is a specialist in a given field, such as construction or education.

A paralegal's work in arbitration includes preparing cases for arbitration, researching arbitration awards, researching contract law and preparing arbitration clauses for insertion into a contract, and sometimes attending an arbitration hearing. Paralegals do not themselves serve as arbitrators unless they have a particular expertise that qualifies them to do so. However, they might find themselves participating as a party in a court-annexed arbitration program.[3]

Attorneys frequently serve as arbitrators, particularly in commercial arbitration. They also prepare cases for arbitration and represent a client at an arbitration hearing. Attorneys may feel more comfortable with arbitration rather than mediation because arbitration is an adjudicatory process that enables them to exercise their adversarial skills.

Like mediation, arbitration can be found in the courts as well as the private sector. Court-annexed arbitration has grown in the last ten years. Yet private arbitration outside of the court system remains an attractive option for some disputants, and there are a number of organizations that are active in the private arbitration field. The American Arbitration Association (AAA), Global Arbitration Mediation Association (GAMA), and Center for Public Resources, Inc. (CPR) are three examples. There is also industry specific arbitration, such as in securities, construction, healthcare, and insurance, among others. Arbitration training, both initial and advanced, is available through a variety of sources. As in mediation, there is presently no licensing or credentialing requirement for arbitrators imposed by the state. Each private sponsoring organization has its own qualifying requirements.

Other Processes

There are other conflict resolution processes available to disputants, both in the court and privately. Many are hybrids or derivations of the procedures named above. They are less pervasive than the three primary processes and are discussed in chapter 6.

---

2 Such requirements usually proceed from the particular state's Rules of Evidence.

3 When a disputant files a court action (i.e., a complaint) to commence litigation, some jurisdictions require the disputants to appear before an arbitrator who will hear their cases and make a binding, or more frequently, nonbinding award.

The Court System

Many disputants take their conflict to the court system for resolution. It remains the primary dispute resolution forum utilized by attorneys. Because each state, as well as the federal government, has its own court system, it is incumbent on the paralegal to be completely familiar with the particular state and federal court system and its practices.[4]

When neighbors fight over a barking dog, one of them will frequently file a complaint[5] in the town or municipal court. If a landlord wants to remove a tenant for failure to pay rent, she will file a complaint in the court that handles landlord/tenant matters. Liability for automobile accidents is usually decided in court. Criminal matters are brought to court by the state on behalf of the injured party. Contract actions, divorce, adoption, negligence, and many other judicially recognized conflicts find their way through our court system each year.

In addition to the trial level, where each party presents her case and the matter is decided by a judge or jury, there is an appellate procedure. This permits certain parties who are not satisfied with the trial court's determination to ask a higher court to review the matter based upon certain prescribed requirements, such as an error of law made by the trial judge.

However, even within the court system, as exemplified by the Federal Rules of Civil Procedure, there is a requirement of a good faith attempt to settle the dispute.[6] Most cases do in fact settle before the actual trial or, as lawyers put it, "on the courthouse steps," and some settle after trial pending appeal. While the judicial system is a dispute resolution system, it will not be studied in depth here because our intent is to review those methods that are an alternative to or complement the court system.

EXERCISES

1. Itemize the conflicts you have had in your life in the past week, whether with individuals, businesses, the government, or similar entities. Next to each conflict indicate what you believe to be the cause and how it was managed, and what you would change in the future and why.

4　The federal and state court systems and the practice within each is beyond the scope of this book.

5　"Filing a complaint" is the manner in which one commences a lawsuit and seeks the intervention of the formal court system.

6　Fed. R. Civ. P. 68.

2. Choose three current conflicts — one on a local level, one on a national level, and the third on an international level. Follow each on the Internet and in the media, and track its progress.

3. Describe the last negotiation in which you participated and how you felt about both the process and the result.

4. Observe and report on a mediation process in your community.

5. Locate the *Labor Arbitration Reports* in your law library and review and report on a recent case.

6. Study the court system within your state. Diagram its structure and briefly describe the jurisdiction (authority) of each court. Then, add to the diagram where ADR is used and for what types of cases.

7. Research what ADR programs are available to attorneys through the state bar association — e.g., fee disputes with clients, breakup of law partnerships, etc.

8. Determine if conflict, conflict management, or dispute resolution is studied elsewhere on your campus or in local colleges or universities and what academic disciplines are offering the coursework or skills training and why.

9. Search for additional industries that use ADR. Develop a class list.

10. Interview someone from another culture about conflict style and write a brief journal about the interview.

11. Brainstorm some ideas for approaching the law office scenario at the beginning of this chapter.

12. Are there any steps the seller can take in the second scenario to minimize his conflict?

Conflict

2

Introduction

What Is Conflict and How Is It Perceived?

Sources of Interpersonal Conflict
 Differences
 Resources
 Miscommunication
 Anger, Mistrust, and Fear
 Responsibility
 Expectations and Roles
 Difficult People

International Conflict

Summary

Exercises

Introduction

Conflict is a normal, healthy, and positive force in everyone's life. It answers to many names and wears diverse faces. Examples include internal conflict that can occur within oneself over simultaneous job offers, within a family over financial matters, within an organization or a business over the breakup of that business, or within a political unit over environmental or spending issues. There is external conflict as well, which occurs between individuals, organizations (or between an individual and an organization), between and among political units, or within the natural environment. Think about examples of each of these. . . . More instances of conflict will come to mind.

Conflicts can be so small that they are hardly noticed or so large that they practically consume the participants, as well as anyone else touched by the conflict. Examples range from divorce to world wars. Most conflicts fall somewhere between these two extremes. In our Western tradition, social interaction almost guarantees periodic conflict.

> [C]onflict plays a central role at all levels of our lives. At the intra personal level, we typically experience conflict each time we make a decision. Over time, these experiences are thought to serve as a foundation of our personalities and self-concepts. Conflict also shadows all of our interpersonal contacts, whether they involve work, play, or love. And as the scope of our interactions expands to include small and large groups, so too does the potential role of conflict expand.[1]

Conflict is a natural state that exists between people and groups, and no matter how hard social scientists try, they will never eliminate or totally resolve it.[2] For example, legal professionals face conflict on a continuing basis, not only through arguing on behalf of a client but by trying to persuade a client to appreciate a certain perspective. Conflicts also occur between attorneys, as well as staff members, within the same firm.

Conflict can be studied from a variety of perspectives. A sociologist will look at a conflict from a social systems context. A political scientist will be interested in "political" conflicts and view them from a historical and political context. A psychologist will study conflict from the perspective of what feelings and emotions brought the parties to the conflict and how their dealing with the conflict will affect their future emotions and feelings. A feminist may see conflict as a power struggle between the sexes and a philosopher will view conflict from an ethical or theoretical point of view. Lawyers

---

1 Stephen Worchel and Jeffrey A. Simpson eds., Conflict Between People and Groups 1 (1993) (citations omitted).

2 *Id.* at 76.

experience conflict in the form of lawsuits and disputes to be resolved within the legal system. There are people who study conflict and its resolution from a scientific, mathematical, and "game" theory perspective.

Similarly, individuals approach conflict from differing personal perspectives. Each person's point of view will depend on his or her emotional and psychological "baggage," life experience and perspective, and educational and cultural background. People are complex, and each disputing party, whether it is an individual or an organization, is complex. Some professionals, such as lawyers, are more comfortable working with conflict, particularly within the context of their profession. Other professional people may be less comfortable with conflict because they are conditioned to avoid or circumvent it.

An in-depth study of conflict will be left to the diverse theorists mentioned above and to others — anthropologists, businesspeople, and clinicians. It is necessary, however, for the student of dispute resolution to expand his or her understanding of conflict and its effect before proceeding to study its resolution. Part of the resolution process is to understand the conflict, its sources, the underlying interests, and the potential for management or resolution.

There is an urgency to the investigation of this topic that results from the "growing presence of conflict in the world. While modern advances in sciences [and technology] have increased our options for travel, lengthened the days of our lives, and given us [greater access to the rest of the world], each of these gains has also provided greater opportunities for conflict to emerge at all levels of our lives."[3] This urgency has spilled over into the legal system, which is expanding the use of dispute resolution to meet the need of increased conflict, both within and outside of the courts.

What Is Conflict and How Is It Perceived?

According to one source, a conflict is "a prolonged battle; a struggle; clash; a controversy; disagreement; opposition."[4] Lawyers define a dispute as "a conflict or controversy; esp. one that has given rise to a particular lawsuit."[5] Most people can define conflict, and more to the point, can think of innumerable examples. Another source states that "conflicts are more than just debates or negotiations. They represent an escalation of everyday competition and discussion into an arena of hostile or

---

3 *Id.* at 2.

4 American Heritage Dictionary of The English Language, (4th ed. 2000).

5 Black's Law Dictionary (8th ed. 2004).

emotion-provoking encounters that strain personal or interpersonal tranquility, or both."[6]

The *Dictionary of Conflict Resolution* has an extensive exploration of "conflict," which should be consulted, but begins with "disagreement or incompatibility. Derived from the Latin conflictus, meaning 'to strike together.' It is used to denote both a process and a state of being."[7]

To many people, conflict has a largely negative connotation. It is considered bad, distasteful, unpleasant, and, to some, it ranks up there right next to "sin." It is certainly true that conflict has the "enormous potential to destroy everything with which it comes in contact."[8] It has led to "war and the buildup of frightening arsenals of weapons. Conflict over values, goals, opportunities, and materials has split apart or destroyed groups."[9]

> Conflict and its most extreme disguise, competition, have been identified as the cause of intergroup hostility, prejudice, and discrimination. The roots of war are often deeply embedded in conflict over territory or basic attitudes and values.[10]

If understood correctly, however, conflict can bear positive fruit. It is an integral and necessary part of life and can be used creatively as a source of clarification, understanding, growth, learning, and communication.

> Conflict plays a positive role at all levels of human interaction (intrapersonal, interpersonal and intergroup). . . . [C]onflict causes the individual to go through a self-examination process. It motivates the individual to mobilize his or her capabilities to deal with or overcome the conflict. Through these efforts the individual becomes better able to define her or his abilities and self-concept.[11]

Conflict is meaningful and, in reality, is a normal response to an issue that is worth struggling over.[12]

---

6   Gini Graham Scott, Disagreements, Disputes, and All Out War 1 (2007).

7   Douglas H. Yarn, ed., Dictionary of Conflict Resolution 113 (1999).

8   Worchel et al, *supra* note 1, at 2.

9   *Id.* at 82.

10   *Id.* at 79 (citations omitted).

11   *Id.* at 78.

12   Forum, National Institute for Dispute Resolution 11.3 (1994).

[C]onflict may [also] initiate broad and important social change. Looking within the United States, open and sometimes violent conflict between blacks and whites served as the stepping stone for reform of nearly every facet of life including education, voting, political districting, employment, law, and even the content of textbooks and popular television programming. Similar reforms can be attributed to conflict between people of different genders, religions, ages, and sexual orientations. It is a matter of speculation whether these changes would have occurred without open confrontation.[13]

The legal system and the professionals who work within it are frequently at the forefront of such changes.

Conflict cannot be ignored. It "demands attention, whether that attention be aimed at removing conflict, resolving it, managing it, or converting it from an evil force into a constructive one."[14] An increase in violence has gained the public's attention, and some see the integration of conflict resolution skills into public education as one response to that violence. An example of this is the development of the peer mediation movement in public schools. In peer mediation, students who have received conflict resolution training and training in mediation skills help other students who are in conflict work through their disputes.

One problem people generally encounter when they address conflict in their lives is that their initial reaction is one of fear. People find themselves overwhelmed and afraid of their own powerful and sometimes irrational feelings.

The difficulty in dealing with conflict is that it touches a part of us that is not purely rational. We each have an emotional and affective side. In conflict this part is roused from its socialized slumber and we feel agitation, anger, even rage. . . . [A] great deal of the powerful energy in conflict arises from the feelings generated, rather than from the purely rational differences involved.[15]

Another problem with conflict is that "adults don't seem to know how to enter into (conflict) with integrity and respect and with some degree of confidence and hope."[16] As a result, many individuals spend a great deal of time and energy either avoiding conflict or avoiding an open discussion of it. "Conflict is the source of all growth and an

---

13 Worchel et al., *supra* note 1, at 79-80.

14 *Id.* at 2.

15 C. James Maselko, The Fair Fight (Effective Aggression) 1 (1985).

16 Selma Myers & Barbara Filner, Mediation Across Cultures: A Handbook about Conflict & Culture 10 (1994).

absolute necessity if one is to be alive. . . . However, unfortunately for too many of us, the idea of conflict is a negative one because we lack the skills to manage disagreements in a healthy, peaceable and respectful way."[17]

> Conflict, intrapersonal, interpersonal, or intergroup, may be uncomfortable, stressful, and followed by destructive consequences. Conflict, itself, is not the smoke that signals that something is amiss within an individual or between individuals. Nor does conflict always require an immediate remedy to reduce its level. Rather, conflict is a natural and necessary part of life and social interaction. It is as likely to initiate deep and positive personal reflection as it is to result in personal distress. It is as likely to motivate growth in a relationship as it is to be a sign of a troubled relationship. And it is as likely to propel group development as it is to instigate intergroup destruction and prejudice.[18]

Mary Parker Follett was businesswoman, community activist, and writer from the early 1900s. She was, among other things, an advocate for creative and constructive approaches conflict resolution. She found that

> "[I]t is often stated that conflict is a necessity of the human soul, and that if conflict should ever disappear from among us, individuals would deteriorate and society collapse. But the effort of agreeing is so much more strenuous than the comparatively easy stunt of fighting that we can harden our spiritual muscles much more effectively on the former than the latter. . . . From war to peace is not from the strenuous to the easy existence; it is from the futile to the effective, from the stagnant to the active, from the destructive to the creative way of life."[19]

If conflict plays a role in creativity, conflict resolution in turn often demands a creative approach, requiring disputants to look beyond their usual mode of response to conflict and to develop new behaviors to achieve a lasting resolution.

> [F]requent conflict . . . can be the sign of a troubled relationship. [However,] numerous investigators have shown that a relationship without conflict, or one in which conflict is avoided, can be equally troubled. . . . Thus, far from being a destroyer, a

---

17   *Id.* at 12.

18   Worchel et al., *supra* note 1, at 88. For an in-depth look at the role of conflict in "group identity and group development," see *id.* at 82-86.

19   J. William Breslin and Jeffery Z. Rubin, eds., Negotiation Theory and Practice. The Program on Negotiation at Harvard Law School 20 (1991).

certain degree of conflict can actually invigorate relationships. In any case, it is not the conflict that is the problem but rather the management and response to conflict that determines the health of the unit. . . . In addition to giving new energy to tired relationships, conflict can serve as a "warning signal" that a relationship is headed for serious problems and identify the nature of the problems.[20]

A reflection of this philosophy is the approach now common among divorce lawyers, who encourage new clients to seek marital counseling before deciding to pursue a divorce.

One must examine the sources of conflict and the bases for them. "Most times it is frustrating because we skip the step of identifying differences and immediately attempt resolution — without knowing what it is we are trying to resolve."[21] One writer theorizes about marital disputes that

> couples should not be too quick to jump into a conflict-resolving mode of behavior. Rather, their first response should be to analyze the conflict and determine the statement it is making about the relationship. . . . Couples are too ready to believe that their fight involves incompatible goals rather than a difference over the means of achieving a common goal.[22]

In addition to studying the conflict, it is important to look at the stage the conflict has reached. Timing may be a critical issue in determining the value of conflict[23] and whether it is an appropriate time to attempt resolution. One must look at whether conflict is serving as a constructive process or as a destructive process. One must guard against "premature resolutions that obscure different interests and perspectives."[24] Conflict should also be "ripe" for resolution, i.e., the parties have more to gain from a resolution than a continuation or escalation of the conflict.

Recent theory suggests that since not all conflict is "resolvable," we must learn to "manage" conflict.

> With proper conflict management skills, potential conflicts can be averted or defused — and even turned into a positive source for improved interpersonal relationships and personal growth. The key is not to avoid conflict, which is

---

20 *Id.* at 78-79.

21 C. James Maselko, Support/Confrontation 5 (1980).

22 Worchel et al., *supra* note 1, at 79.

23 *Id.* at 89.

24 Forum, National Institute for Dispute Resolution 5 (1994).

potentially inherent in all social interaction and in all personal choices we make, but to recognize it and manage it skillfully to produce the best outcome.[25]

Sources of Interpersonal Conflict

There are innumerable sources of conflict, which include differences; limited resources; miscommunication, misunderstanding, or misperception; anger, mistrust, and fear; thwarted expectations and changing roles; and "difficult people."[26]

Differences

The differences between individuals, organizations, and nations are a common source of conflict. Indeed, conflict may be inevitable because of our differences. While differences can be enriching, they can also cause alienation, isolation, and conflict. What are some of our differences?

> [A]ge, sex, race, ethnicity, language, education, social status, economic status, geographic community, verbal and non-verbal expressions, hierarchy, manners, religion and spirituality, symbols, social control mechanisms, conformity/ individuality, conceptions of the "self," expressions of emotions, fatalism/ self-determinism, the role of sexual orientation, beliefs about fairness, honesty, and truth, conceptions of time, face-saving, uses of ritual and of course, beliefs about conflict.[27]

These are but representative examples. The general point is that sometimes, when we are in conflict, we are "simply making explicit the differences that exist between us."[28]

Some of the differences that have been mentioned can be characterized as cultural. That raises the question as to what constitutes "culture."

> A narrow concept of "culture" includes what most of us think of immediately: elements such as nationality, ethnicity, language, religion. But while researchers

---

25 Scott, *supra* note 6, at 2.

26 See also *infra*, page 31.

27 Judith A. Kruger & Michelle LeBaron Duryea, The Tapestry of Culture: A Design for the Assessment of Intercultural Disputes, 68 *in* Taking Stock, 1992 Proceedings of 20th Annual Conference of Society of Professionals in Dispute Resolution (Oct. 1992).

28 Maselko, *supra* note 21, at 4.

do not agree on one definition of culture, there is a general consensus that a broad definition of culture is needed that takes into account demographic variables, status variables, and affiliation variables.[29]

Cultural differences, then, go far beyond race, religion, nationality, or gender.

> [L]imiting consideration to objective culture (visible culture that can be identified from inside or outside of the group, such as language or nationality) without consideration of subjective culture (internalized attitudes, assumptions, opinions, and feelings held by group members) can dangerously create or reinforce stereotypes, and shut down what should be a permanent, fluid learning process.[30]

Again, cultural diversity refers to more than race, ethnicity, or gender. It includes age, lifestyles, sexual orientations, contrasting abilities and skills, and other factors that "influence peoples' beliefs, values, assumptions and, in turn, their communication styles."[31] "We would define culture more informally as a set of rules, written and unwritten, which instruct individuals on how to operate effectively with one another and with their environment. It not only defines ways to act, but also ways to react, and thus is a valuable tool."[32]

Members of different cultures vary even in the way they attempt to persuade others to their position.

> In some cultures it is acceptable to marshal forcefully, but truthfully, all the arguments for one's own side and to avoid giving gratuitous help to the other side. In other cultures it is acceptable to exaggerate or even to bend the truth here and there—but not too much. In still other cultures a really big whopper, if accomplished with flair and humor, is something to brag about and not to hide after the fact, especially if it is successful.[33]

The legal profession itself is a form of a "culture." Legal personnel use a unique language and understand the legal arena of courts, contests, and conflict in a way that laypersons do not. They often deal with people in conflict and under stress. As a result,

---

29   Kruger & Duryea, *supra* note 27, at 66.

30   *Id.* at 67.

31   Myers & Filner, *supra* note 16, at 35.

32   *Id.* at 34.

33   Howard Raiffa, The Art and Science of Negotiation 47 (1982). Reprinted 2005.

lawyers are frequently disliked or misunderstood by the general public; they are stereo-typed, giving rise to many "anti-lawyer" jokes.

Think about all the things that contribute to making you a unique individual and how they could be considered part of your "culture." Given all of these characteristics that define who you are, stereotyping might seem like a natural result. However, one must assiduously avoid stereotyping, which can itself lead to conflict. Further,

> [o]ne must be cautious in classifying every dispute as cultural. It may simply be a personality clash between two individuals who dislike each other, or for whom the chemistry does not work. Even in such apparently non-cultural situations, the conflict may be exacerbated by cultural behaviors. . . . More difficult to identify are conflicts which arise from basic non-cultural issues, which somehow become overlaid with cultural differences originating from values, beliefs and attitudes. Because culture is so deeply ingrained, individuals make cultural assumptions and may not be aware their assumptions are being challenged. Variations from the norm are often misjudged to be deviations.[34]

Some examples of differences that can create or exacerbate conflict include differing communication styles, differing attitudes toward conflict itself, differing levels of respect for others (such as the aged), and differing values placed on assertiveness and individual rights. For example, in the dominant United States culture, individualism is valued and independence in decision-making is important. In other cultures, the group is considered more important than the individual, and the desire for harmony exceeds the desire for individual recognition. In some cultural environments, physical closeness and direct eye contact is the norm while in others it is considered offensive or disrespectful. Some groups place significant emphasis on the present and the future, while others hold the past in greater reverence.

Although individual and cultural differences are an important source of conflict and it is therefore essential to be aware of them, they should not be overemphasized. One must keep in mind the similarities shared by diverse cultures and the universal aspects of all humanity, including our need to belong, thrive, and protect our family. It has been said that we have much more in common than our differences would tell.

Resources

Limited resources are an obvious source of conflict. When there is "too little to go around," individuals, communities, states, businesses, and nations will vie over the

---

34 Myers & Filner, *supra* note 16, at 15.

available resources. Such competition is a major source of business for attorneys. A significant dispute resolution skill is to enlarge the "pie" over which the disputants are competing. This, however, cannot always be done and conflicts ranging from arguments to wars result.

Disputants may also need to differentiate between needs and wants to determine what is necessary and what is desirable. When resources are limited, the parties must attempt to "satisfy as best as possible each person's highest priorities or most important needs in return for getting concessions on lower priority items or needs . . . or . . . try to find new alternative positions that provide good payoffs for both."[35] Some conflicts arising from limited resources are not capable of being resolved in the traditional way and the parties must creatively devise a process for dealing with future conflicts.

Miscommunication

Failure of communication, incomplete communication, or incorrect communication are significant sources of conflict. If a communication is not understood, or only conveys part of the necessary information, or requires assumptions to be made by the listener, or is not made at all, conflict is a highly probable result. For example, if a teenager forgets to tell his parents that after the football game there is a party that he intends to attend and then arrives home very late, causing his parents to worry about safety, his failure to communicate is at least one of the sources of the ensuing conflict. If his parents then fail to effectively communicate to him that their anger arises from their concern for him, he may assume or believe that they just do not want him to grow up, or be independent, or have fun. If the teenager then storms out of the house in anger, the parents may assume he is being rebellious, when he is just venting his anger and giving himself time to cool down. And on . . . and on . . . and on. Similar miscommunications occur on all levels of personal interaction.

There is a communication strategy for dealing with such conflicts as above that encourages dialogue between the parties, rather than blaming and creating angry, inadequate communication. The strategy involves the use of "I messages." A speaker can say "I feel (name an emotion), when (something happens) because (why the speaker feels that way)." This is sometimes followed by an invitation to joint problem solving, such as "what can we do about this?" Applied to the above scenario with the teenager, the parent might say, "I feel worried when I don't know where you are because I care about you. What can we do to avoid this situation in the future?" By using this strategy the speaker owns the emotion, states the cause and why she feels that way, rather than

---

35 *Id.* at 157.

blaming the other party. Such blaming will likely result in disrupted communication and anger, rather than dialogue, which is intended to resolve the situation.

> Communication, the key to resolving most conflicts, is itself often the cause of conflict. Any breakdown of communication can lead to conflict; and there are numerous examples in everyday interactions. Sometimes one person isn't clear. Sometimes someone isn't listening. There are often misunderstandings about meanings. Hidden assumption can stand in the way. And sometimes there is no communication at all, resulting in misunderstandings, hostility, or resentment.[36]

One must bear in mind that communication is nonverbal as well as verbal. An individual may say one thing, but convey something else through nonverbal communication.

> Experts in the communication field tell us that we get about 55 percent of our information from the non-verbal communication that accompanies a spoken message (such as facial gestures and body movements). We get about 38 percent from the voice, pitch, tone, and sounds we hear; and only 7 percent from content. This means that we're remarkably likely to misinterpret or discredit the very message someone thinks he or she is communicating.[37]

Consider a co-worker who says "good morning" with a frown on his face. Isn't this likely to cause confusion, incorrect assumptions, or anger in the listener?

Simply and concisely put, the best way to deal with miscommunication, or lack of communication is to *communicate*, discuss what is unclear, make sure all participants understand each other, and listen effectively.

A significant part of communication is listening. People are not taught how to be effective listeners and tend to take the skill of listening for granted. However, listening is very important. First, it is necessary to actually pay attention to the speaker, not be distracted by TV, other people, or one's own thoughts. For example, people frequently listen to the first part of what someone says and then stop listening to formulate a response to what the other person said, rather than listening to the second part of the communication. Second, an effective listener makes eye contact and demonstrates empathy through nonverbal behaviors. Third, it is important for the listener to be supportive in verbal responses, and to not offer advice (unless requested), change the

---

36   Scott, *supra* note 6, at 99.

37   *Id.* at 100.

subject, or judge the speaker. Too often we think someone is seeking our help or advice, so we provide it, without making sure that is what is being requested. Finally, if necessary, the listener should seek clarification through nonjudgmental questions. Why this emphasis on "nonjudgmental"? Quite simply, the speaker is seeking to be heard, not judged.

Anger, Mistrust, and Fear

Other sources of conflict are anger, mistrust, and fear, which occur in most relationships. Each of these emotions can build up over time, especially if not recognized and dealt with directly when it first appears. In a relationship,

> [t]here can be real hurts, imagined hurts, and new hurts on top of past hurts, which keep mounting up. . . . [E]ach person thinks the other is acting out of bad will, and sees each new action, no matter how innocent, as another attack. Mistrust can be real or imagined. Fears can be rational or irrational, but they can interfere with a relationship and cause conflict. Conflicts often arise when people have underlying needs or strong wants that aren't being met, such as a desire for security, perhaps independence, or belonging. Conflicts also grow out of fears that something valuable may be lost: a friendship, property, peace and quiet.[38]

Issues of anger, mistrust, and fear are best dealt with by confronting the feelings, discussing the feelings, and deciding whether the parties want to continue the relationship or end it. Without confronting the anger or mistrust, and thereby giving the parties an opportunity to express their feelings and to dissipate them, the relationship will continue to be unsatisfactory. Fear needs to be dealt with more sensitively, by attempting to recognize the fear in oneself or others, understanding that fear, and helping to alleviate it.

How can we confront these emotional barriers to harmony? One source indicates that we need to learn how to support another person *and* confront him at the same time.

> Support is accepting as valid for the other person whatever s/he says, thinks, feels, believes irrespective of my agreement. To accept as valid how the other perceives reality even though I do not share that view. Support is always for the other. It allows the other to be heard and understood, not necessarily agreed with.[39]

---

38 Scott, *supra* note 6, at 69.

39 Maselko, *supra* note 21, at 2.

Most people need to be heard more than they need to have someone agree with them. It is an affirmation of their reality.

Facing conflict can result in confrontation. Confrontation is risky, but failure to confront is also risky because nothing changes. The "skill of confrontation is the ability to make explicit the differences between us without negating your position as valid for you. It requires me to acknowledge your position and differentiate yours from mine. The skill allows the differences to be clarified and explored prior to any attempt at problem solving."[40] This skill, along with enhanced communication skills, is essential in dealing with many of the sources of conflict covered in this chapter.

Responsibility

Misunderstandings and misperceptions can result from miscommunication. They can also result from conflict over shared responsibility — someone taking on too much responsibility or too little responsibility.

> These extremes in taking or giving responsibility can produce conflict because of the reaction they produce in others. When one person fails to take responsibility, others can resent being left with the blame or the work; while when someone takes on too much responsibility for something, and perhaps too much of the credit, others can feel resentful or alienated.[41]
>
> In one common situation, a person takes on extra responsibility because he or she doesn't think the other person is taking on enough. The other person is often unaware of the need for that responsibility. That person might also have different priorities, or might not see what has to be done since it is being done by the first person. This is a frequent source of conflict between husband and wife.[42]

Picture a situation in which there are two administrative assistants in a department. One always seems to have the responsible jobs, while the other seldom seems to work very hard. The one who has the responsible jobs feels important, but overworked. The individual who does not appear to be working hard may be fearful of responsibility and may resent the other. This situation is bound to result in conflict. The parties need to explore the realities of the conflict and develop a working relationship that will be responsive to both of their needs, as well as to those of their employer. This requires

---

40 *Id.* at 6.

41 Scott, *supra* note 6, at 49.

42 *Id.* at 60.

effective communication and each party's being open about their feelings. Only then can they develop a plan to avoid the "responsibility trap" in the future.

Expectations and Roles

Thwarted expectations and the way roles change can best be explained in the marital context. Each spouse comes from a unique family and has certain expectations based upon his or her own family experience. But because both spouses are different from their parents and each marriage is therefore unique, it is practically impossible to duplicate a marriage that one saw (or believed they saw) as a child. To further complicate the issue of expectations, the roles of men and women in marriage are evolving. A man whose father "ruled the house" may feel emasculated when he does not wield the same authority or receive the same expression of respect that his father did. Likewise, a woman whose mother did not work outside of the home and was able to expend all her energy on homemaking may feel like society and her husband demand too much of her, expecting her to have a career and maintain a home at the same time. Imagine two professionals (doctors, lawyers, etc.) who are married to one another, each accustomed to having people (patients, clients) listen to them and take their advice. To extend such expectations to their respective spouses will cause immediate and long-term conflict.

Similar conflicts can occur in the workplace. People accuse assertive women of being too aggressive, or individuals may have difficulty working for someone from an ethnic group they thought to be undeserving of such authority. As an example, it is only in the last 30 years that women and minorities have established their presence in the legal profession. An older secretary who has always worked for an older white male may resent a new attorney who is younger, or female, or from a racial minority. Any shift of roles and expectations can cause conflict.

A person needs to be realistic about the expectations he has of himself as well as of others. Such realism will contribute greatly toward avoiding conflicts based on faulty or outdated or unrealistic expectations. Further, each party to a conflict must see the other as a unique individual or entity, and not relate to the other on the basis of the "role" he is assumed to perform. If this is done and communication is open, the parties can explore together the inaccurate assumptions that lead to conflict.

Difficult People

Some people are just difficult! They can be hostile, naysayers, know-it-alls, etc. To make this issue more complex, each of us reacts differently to different kinds of difficult people, i.e., some people are more able than others to "push our buttons" through their behavior. Some people despise liars, others abhor really aggressive individuals, and still others cannot deal with indecisive people.

The problem is not identifying difficult people but dealing with them. It has been suggested that an individual (1) work through one's own emotional charges triggered by difficult people and (2) try to determine why they are being difficult.[43] The latter is accomplished through effective communication. "[M]ost people are difficult because they have certain underlying needs or interests that they meet by acting that way. . . . Thus, if you decide it's worth it to deal with people who are difficult, you might look for these underlying needs and think of how you can satisfy them."[44]

We must also learn not to take other people's behavior personally. "[A]nother person's negative or provoking behavior is often not directed specifically at you. The other person might have a problem; it has nothing to do with you, so why take it on?"[45] This may be the secret technique used by an employee who is able to work with an employer no one else can stand because he is so difficult.

International Conflict

International conflicts can be seen as internal, regional, or wars between states. Internal conflicts occur within a nation, involving civil war between opposing groups or between a group and the existing government, or when a particular nation has become a failed state, i.e., has no rule of law, extensive civil rights abuses, etc. Civil wars can be of relatively short duration or long-term (over several generations) and seemingly intractable.

Regional conflict is often the result of the spilling over of a civil or internal conflict into a region, as well as power struggles within a region or conflicts between different ethnic and/or religious groups within a region. There are always examples of regional conflict in the international news.

International conflicts are very complex and evolve over time. They require a multi-tiered approach to resolution, including diplomacy, social and economic support, and sometimes restraint through armed force by a group of outside nations. Failed states in particular require the very long-term commitment of outsiders combined with the involvement of the citizens of that state.

There are a great number of resources on this subject, but it is recommended to start with the United States Institution of Peace (http://www.usip.org) and the information available there, as well as a news organization with an international focus, such as the British Broadcasting Corporation (http://www.bbc.co.uk).

---

43   *Id.* at 182.

44   *Id.* at 180.

45   *Id.* at 35.

Summary

Conflict is a natural occurrence and an integral part of everyone's life. It can be internal or external, brief or ongoing, personal or group conflict. It is a powerful positive force contributing to change and growth, requiring attention and a creative response. It is important to understand conflict and its source prior to attempting to resolve conflict. As a society, we need to develop effective conflict management skills as well as techniques for conflict resolution.

There are many sources of conflict. The differences between and among individuals, groups, and nations can lead to misunderstanding, apprehension, fear, and stereotyping. While one must be aware of the differences and how they contribute to conflict, one also must be careful to not stereotype or see cultural differences as the cause of every conflict.

Limited resources can cause conflict even among friends and family. Consider its effect on an already strained relationship or among strangers. Parties must work to expand resources, seek to obtain only their highest priority items, or creatively share in order to avoid continuous vying and antagonism. Collaboration toward enhancing future resources might also be in order.

Miscommunication is one of the most significant sources of conflict. It is effectively remedied, however, through recognition of the miscommunication by sharpening our communication and addressing any communication failure.

In order to understand conflict, one must be able to recognize anger, mistrust, and fear in oneself as well as others. Then one needs to confront these feelings in oneself, or, if they emanate from someone else, discuss with them the feelings and be supportive. This supportive attitude is really communicating that one hears and understands the other, which can be done without necessarily agreeing with the other.

How much responsibility one takes on can also be a source of conflict. Some individuals accept too much responsibility and later resent it; others accept too little responsibility and are resented. The best way to deal with these issues is to recognize them and openly discuss them so that the responsibility can be shared in a manner acceptable to all involved.

Unmet expectations and changing roles frequently contribute to conflict. Expectations, realistic or otherwise, are usually not communicated and frustration and anger result when they are not met. Once again, one must engage in a critical look at one's expectations and role stereotypes and, if appropriate, share one's perspectives on these issues with the other person.

We all know someone who could be described as "difficult." And, politically, we may have definite ideas about which nations we have an uneasy alliance with.

Frequently, individuals and nations are "difficult" because they have unmet needs. If one chooses to deal with them, or must deal with them, it is best to determine what those unmet needs are.

There is a three-step pattern here that deserves attention. In most conflict situations, one must ferret out and understand the source of the conflict, realistically analyze it, and communicate effectively about it. This three-step analysis should be directed to oneself as well as to one's relationship with others. Before we blame others for the conflict, we should first look at ourselves.

EXERCISES

1. Maintain a weekly conflict journal, in which you describe at least one personal conflict for each week and indicate what you believe the source of the conflict was, whether it was resolved, how it was resolved, and how you feel about the conflict and its resolution or nonresolution.

2. Choose one of the conflict sources covered in this chapter and create a scenario demonstrating how it works to create conflict.

3. Locate, read, and report on a scholarly article about conflict from another academic perspective, e.g., anthropology, sociology, math, psychology, history, or philosophy.

4. Describe how you feel when you are in conflict with someone and how you believe the other person feels. Describe how you feel when you observe others in conflict.

5. Find and report on a historic example of how conflict was productive and brought about positive change.

6. In an ongoing relationship, how would you manage the negative part of conflict and give the positive side an opportunity to expand?

7. Describe a conflict (yours or someone else's) in which you believe that the failure to effectively communicate was one of the sources of the conflict.

8. Describe two families (e.g., neighbors, in-laws, etc.) you have observed in a relationship with each other, and indicate how their respective family cultures differed. Overall, did these differences enrich the relationship or cause conflict, or both?

9. Read and report on a scholarly or business article describing how communication styles differ according to nation of origin; for example, differing communication styles between Japanese and American businesspeople.

10. Practice being supportive of another without necessarily agreeing with their point of view. Describe how you did this and the result. Do this several times and determine if this is an aid in conflict management and resolution.

11. List your expectations of this class; describe how the reality of the class differs from your expectations.

12. Read different perspectives regarding a current national or international conflict and try to determine its source.

Negotiation

Essential Steps in the Process
  Preliminary Negotiations
  Central Negotiations
  Closing of Negotiations
  Other Factors
  Summary

Communication Skills
  Verbal Communication
  Listening Skills
  Nonverbal Communication
  Other Issues

Applications
  Professional Fulfillment
  On Behalf of the Employer
  Rulemaking Negotiation

Ethics
  Ethical Rules
  Representative Conflict
  Truth
  A Higher Standard
  Confidentiality

Exercises

Negotiation Role Plays
  A Family in Crisis (three parties)
  Office Injustices (five parties)
  The Computer System (two parties)
  The Japanese Businessman (two parties)

Introduction

Negotiation is defined in several ways: "The deliberation, discussion, or conference upon the terms of a proposed agreement; the act of settling or arranging the terms and conditions of a bargain, sale, or other business transaction."[1] Or, "bilateral or multilateral process in which parties who differ over a particular issue attempt to reach agreement or compromise over that issue through communication."[2] Or, to negotiate is "to hold communication or conference (with another) for the purpose of arranging some matter by mutual agreement; to discuss a matter, with a view to some settlement or compromise."[3] Some would say that negotiation is really the act of attempting to persuade others to adopt your point of view.

Everyone negotiates—friends, enemies, and strangers alike. Children negotiate amongst themselves over family responsibilities; commuters negotiate over who will drive to work; students negotiate study assignments; spouses negotiate with each other daily; consumers negotiate to purchase a car or a house; and employees and employers negotiate over salary and benefits. Governments and organizations negotiate through various representatives regarding economic, political, and social issues. Negotiation is carried on face-to-face, over the telephone, in writing, over e-mail, in chat rooms, through video conferencing, and through third parties. Negotiation, in one form or another, is an integral part of our lives.

Is negotiation a skill that can be learned, a science that may be predicted, or an art practiced only by those people who have the gift? There are elements of all three in negotiation; but learning the skills and techniques, engaging in appropriate preparation, understanding the process, studying the theory and applications, and, of course, practice all aid in the development of a more sophisticated and informed negotiating ability.

Negotiation Theories

Competitive Approach

There are a number of approaches to negotiation. One is the competitive, "all-for-me" approach. The *Dictionary of Conflict Resolution* at page 93, defines competing as "both assertive and uncooperative. Competing individuals pursue their own concerns without regard for others' interests and use whatever power seems appropriate to win (citations omitted)." In the extreme, the negotiator is attempting to win as much as

---

1   Black's Law Dictionary (8th ed. 2004).

2   Douglas H. Yarn, ed., Dictionary of Conflict Resolution, 314 (1991).

3   Oxford English Dictionary 303 (2d ed. 2005).

possible, regardless of the cost. If winning is the sole criterion, this type of negotiator is frequently successful, because a competitive negotiator can frequently overpower and overwhelm an opponent. However, this approach may also result in failure because it inflames the other side or pushes so hard that no agreement is reached. Or an agreement may be reached, but subsequently not honored; an agreement that someone is badgered into accepting is less likely to be honored than one that is reached as a result of everyone's active participation. Another negative result of overly competitive behavior is the reputation the negotiator develops, which may make future negotiations more difficult.

Cooperative Approach

A different approach to negotiation is the cooperative/collaborative one, sometimes called the "win-win" approach of Fisher and Ury's *Getting to Yes*.[4] A cooperative strategy is defined in the *Dictionary of Conflict Resolution* at page 132 "as an affirmative negotiation technique in which a negotiator grants unilateral concessions so as to establish a relationship built on trust and to create a moral obligation for the other side to reciprocate with similar concessions." Negotiators are encouraged to attempt to get beyond positional bargaining ("This is what I want and that is that!") and determine the underlying interests of each party so that they can creatively fashion an agreement that is more likely to meet all the parties' needs. One technique used in cooperative negotiation, consists of rather than dividing up an existing pie, the negotiators expand the pie. If a municipality received an arts grant that was insufficient to meet the basic needs of the arts organizations in town, they could fight over this limited resource, or they could collaborate to apply for additional grants and thereby "expand the pie," or gather more funding to divide among them. While such an approach cannot work in all situations — it would not be applicable, for example, where price is the only issue — the techniques and attitudes of the cooperative approach provide a more congenial environment for any type of negotiation.

The ultimate goal is to maximize everyone's opportunity for gain:

> Searching for joint gains should be distinguished from compromising, which requires that everyone give up something. The goal in collaborative negotiation is to find solutions that satisfy everyone's interests, not to leave everyone with less than was hoped. "Splitting the difference" in compromise merely distributes the pain of losing — and often rewards the more unreasonable bargainer to boot.[5]

---

4 Roger Fisher and William Ury, Getting To Yes (2d ed. 1991).

5 Linda R. Singer, Settling Disputes: Conflict Resolution in Business, Families, and The Legal System 17 (2d ed. 1994).

Distributive vs. Integrative Bargaining

Single-issue negotiation, in which it is not possible to expand the field of issues, suggests the need for distributive bargaining, i.e., "more for me is less for you." Multiple-issue negotiation calls for integrative bargaining, i.e., a trading of issues and ordering of priorities. Sometimes a single-issue problem can be enlarged to include additional issues.

> Frequently the parties to a negotiation can do better by elaborating the problem and converting a single-factor negotiating problem into a multiple-factor problem. Often the motivation to do so is the fact that without this type of elaboration no agreement can be reached, and the bargaining principals may feel uncomfortable about not reaching an agreement.[6]

Transactional vs. Problem-Solving Negotiation

This text addresses largely conflict or problem-solving negotiation, in which the parties have, or have had, differences and are communicating to resolve those differences. However, there is a great deal of negotiating that occurs for parties to enter into a new relationship or contract, which is not based on a prior conflict. In this type of negotiation, both parties want this new relationship and are using negotiation to develop its foundation. There is greater potential for rancor in a problem-solving scenario than in a transactional scenario. By way of example, when parties negotiate to enter into a contract for the sale of a boat, one to the other, it is a transactional negotiation. If, however, one of the parties breaches that contract, perhaps by not purchasing the boat, or the seller misrepresenting the quality of the boat, they will enter into a problem-solving negotiation to determine breach, liability, and damages, if any.

Linking Issues

A technique commonly used to create or enlarge the issues in a negotiation is linkage. Here, the parties agree to future relations, such as future working arrangements and/or contracts. An agreement to provide future contracts links the successful negotiation of the current contract or dispute to expanded business between the parties, thereby providing for tradeoffs.

---

6   Howard Raiffa, The Art & Science of Negotiation 102 (1982). Reprinted 2005.

Flexibility

A good negotiator will be able to combine the strategies of the various negotiation styles and be flexible enough to determine the optimum use of each. A good negotiator must be well prepared, but must also be flexible when new information is gained that affects the negotiator's prior perspective on the situation. The negotiator must be able to assess and apply the new information quickly, sometimes during the actual negotiation. In addition, a good negotiator will know herself, i.e., have a realistic understanding of her own abilities and the style with which she is most comfortable.[7] A negotiator is most effective when acting in a manner that is consistent with her personality and preferences regarding human interaction.

Examples

What are the differences between competitive and cooperative approaches in an actual negotiation? Let us look at a transactional negotiation. Assume an individual needs to purchase a used car for work and school. He has saved $1,500 and does not want to pay more than that because his job is too insecure to justify getting involved in monthly payments. A "friend-of-a-friend" is selling a five-year-old compact car with high mileage. She is asking $2,000 for it. The friend indicates that as far as he knows, the owner has had no accidents and no significant mechanical problems with the car. The buyer could approach the situation by telling the owner everything he thinks is wrong with the car and saying it is not worth more than $1,000. This reflects a competitive approach. Conversely, he could discuss what the "blue book" value is, what his needs are, and what he is able to afford, while trying to find out what the seller's needs are. Does she need the money from this car as a down payment on another car? Is she leaving the area, or for some reason no longer needs a car? For both parties to work together to meet both their needs reflects a cooperative approach.

Dealing only with the issue of price would be a distributive stance and might result in no bargain being struck. However, after talking with each other for some time, the parties might discover that the car owner is having computer problems in her business and the purchaser is a computer whiz. An exchange for value could be made wherein the purchaser would provide future computer troubleshooting services to the seller in exchange for a lowering in the price of the automobile now. This approach reflects the use of linkage and an integrative approach.

---

7   There is a computer program, called "Negotiator Pro," that helps one undertake the sort of self analysis that is helpful here. *http://www.negotiatorpro.com.*

One-Text Approach

A third approach to negotiation is called the one-text approach. Here, one party or a neutral third party offers a single proposal dealing with all the issues between the disputants. Then, the next party modifies the proposal and passes it on to the next party (if there is one) for further modification, until all parties have had their input. This process continues until the disputants reach a consensus on the total package. The one-text approach has the benefit of focusing on the dispute and using a joint effort to reach a resolution, rather than focusing on the differences between the parties. This approach is especially beneficial in multi-party negotiations, which "are often too diffuse to be effective unless they focus on a single negotiating text."[8] Sometimes the text is proposed by an intervenor. For an example of such an approach, look at a discussion of the Camp David negotiations in Howard Raiffa's *The Art & Science of Negotiation*.[9]

Theory Summary

There are two basic approaches to bargaining: competitive and cooperative. The competitive approach has historically been favored by attorneys, who bargain very hard to get the most for their clients. Current theory, however, supports the cooperative approach in order for both parties to achieve the maximum joint gains. A negotiator should be sufficiently flexible to employ a combination of both to achieve the best outcome. Distributive versus integrative bargaining is a comparison of negotiation based upon the number of issues. In distributive bargaining, it is best to expand the issues so that integrative bargaining can occur. Transactional negotiation creates a contract between the parties, such as a "buy-sell," while problem-solving negotiation addresses disputes between the parties. Linkage is a vehicle whereby the negotiation is linked to future dealings between the parties, thereby expanding the issues.

The one-text approach to bargaining occurs when all issues are joined in one solution and the solution is then modified until the parties find the total package acceptable.

Preparation for Negotiation

Most successful activity requires preparation. Negotiation is no different. Clearly, the preparation necessary or possible will vary depending on the situation. However, preparedness, mixed with flexibility, benefits even the most skilled negotiator. How can one best prepare?

---

8   Raiffa, *supra* note 6, at 254.

9   *Id.* at 205.

Factual Preparation

Obtain all the factual information possible about the product or conflict, the people, your position and interests, the other side's position and interests, the market, and your alternatives. For example, Hannah, a college student, is moving to the town in which her college is located and wants to rent a room or apartment off-campus. She has looked at two apartments advertised in the newspaper and she likes one of them but does not feel she can afford the rent of $700 per month. She will be meeting with the landlord soon to negotiate an agreement. How can she prepare for this transactional negotiation?

Hannah can investigate other rentals by contacting a local realtor, which will provide a better picture of the local market. She can compare this with on-campus housing by speaking with the college housing office. She can also speak with other students to gain their perspective. Then she can speak with tenants in the building in which she wishes to rent in order to gather information regarding the landlord and the apartment building. She might also ask to see a copy of the landlord's lease ahead of time so that she can review it at her own pace. Information about the security of the area can be learned by contacting the police.

In addition, Hannah may need to review her own budget and additional funding sources that are available. She must determine the highest amount she can afford to pay for rent. Can she get a job on campus or near the apartment? Should she consider sharing with a roommate? She should contact the financial aid office regarding those resources. Hannah must also project what the landlord's interests may be. How long has the apartment been vacant? Are there other apartments in the building that are vacant? Is the property maintained well? Consider whether the landlord might exchange services, such as lawn care and snow removal, for a percentage of the rent.[10]

Role-Playing

In addition to factual preparation, preparing for negotiation should also include role-playing. In such a simulation, two or more individuals will act out the negotiation, trying out various case scenarios and playing both sides of the conflict. This increases one's confidence and comfort level with the process, aids in strategizing, and permits experimentation with various negotiation styles.

One might also seek the services of a negotiation coach as part of preparing for a negotiation. A coach will focus the person on issues, goals, risks, and interests, and all the items referred to herein.

---

10   For an excellent example of factual and tactical preparation for negotiation, flexibility during negotiation, and the results, see the description of the negotiation regarding Elmtree House in *id.* at 35-43.

Other Determinations

In addition to factual preparation, the party must determine who is the best negotiator — the party himself, an attorney, or some other representative. If the party is actually a group of people, such as a school or synagogue, should the negotiator be someone in the group with experience in negotiation, someone in the group with experience related to the subject matter of the dispute, someone with past experience dealing with the other party, or an outsider to represent the group?

Preparation includes the negotiator knowing himself, his needs, and his best alternative to a negotiated agreement (BATNA). It includes analyzing goals or aspiration levels and placing a value on them, searching for alternatives, setting the reservation price, and developing and organizing arguments. Goals or aspiration levels represent the optimum settlement for a party. Valuation of them has to do with "deciding what one wants . . . and what they would be willing to give up in order to achieve their goal. One approach is to try to generate scoring systems that assign points to various levels within each attribute and that quantify tradeoffs between issues."[11] Reservation price is the absolute minimum that a negotiating party will accept. When an agreement isn't reached even after resorting to one's reservation price, one should have an idea of a preferred BATNA, which is what one would want to happen when the disputants fail to settle.

Preparation also includes analyzing the other disputants, their potential goals, reservation price, BATNA, and negotiating style. Finally, one should be aware of the negotiating customs of the country, region, or industry and of the parties. For example, is lying considered extreme exaggeration or withholding information, and is it acceptable behavior in this type of negotiation?

Time, Place, and Parties

Prior to the actual meeting, the parties should set a time and place for the negotiation. The time should be mutually agreed upon and location can be at a neutral site or at one of the party's place of business. It should be a place where all parties are comfortable, private, and where interruption can be kept to a minimum. Who should participate in the negotiation is a more complex issue. While the identity of the parties in a two-party dispute may be clear, they may want to bring a family member or community elder to the negotiation. To exclude them might have a negative impact on the disputant's ability to effectively participate in the negotiation; to permit a nonparty to be present, however, may alter the power balance. In a dispute over an environmental issue, on the other hand, even identifying all the parties in interest is

---

11 *Id.* at 148.

difficult. Questions arise as to what special interest groups should be involved and who will protect the interests of the public. Sometimes the field of potential parties is too broad; the issue as to who attends the negotiation may therefore become one of the issues to be negotiated.

Flexibility

This bears repeating: flexibility is essential. It requires the negotiator to periodically reassess her interests and positions and the projected interests and positions of the other party based upon information acquired during negotiation. Flexibility also requires the negotiator to remain open to new ideas and suggestions that may come from the other side. It is helpful to view the negotiation as an opportunity for an exchange of ideas and options looking toward joint gains, rather than a struggle to obtain one's own desired outcome.

Essential Steps in the Process

After thorough preparation, establishing the meeting place, and determining who will participate, the actual negotiating meeting takes place. While negotiations can and do take place over the telephone, a face-to-face meeting allows the parties to observe each other's nonverbal communication during negotiation, encourages total concentration without distraction, and demonstrates a commitment to the process. However, face-to-face negotiations are not always possible and other means — telephonic, electronic, paper, etc. — are required. At the meeting, some negotiators will want to get the easy issues out of the way first and get the parties in an "agreeing" frame of mind. Others may want to tackle the most difficult areas first. Some negotiators will establish an agenda of the issues to be covered, while others want to leave the structure more free-flowing. In this respect, there is no right or wrong way. It will depend on the negotiators, the parties, the time frame, the subject of the negotiation, and the tradition of negotiation in the field.

Preliminary Negotiations

"Opening gambits" — the first steps taken in the negotiation process — involve finding out more about the other side's positions, confirming facts, introducing outside standards, and perhaps making initial offers. Some negotiators are more willing to provide factual information than others. Obtaining as much factual information as possible is essential to an informed negotiation and settlement. The use of outside standards (e.g., using an independent appraisal of real estate to establish value or using the "blue book" value for automobiles) has a neutralizing effect. Each negotiator should try to explore the other party's underlying interests and cautiously convey her own. Opening offers should be neither too extreme nor too conservative. This may also be an opportunity to learn more about the other negotiators.

Central Negotiations

The next step of formal negotiations has been called the "negotiation dance." This is where collaborative problem solving becomes so important. Once negotiations begin in earnest, it is important to be aware of concessions, how frequently they are made, and how much is conceded in each. The rate of concessions may increase as parties near an agreement. There may be some trading of issues: one party may feel intractable on one issue, but is willing to concede on another. These must be explored. Concessions made by one side are usually linked to the other party's concessions. If an impasse is reached on one issue, move on to the next and return to the impasse later.

Brainstorming can be helpful in this stage. It allows the parties to offer suggestions without being committed to them. "Negotiations are most productive when parties feel comfortable inventing solutions without committing to them — at least not until all possible outcomes have been identified and evaluated."[12] Issue clarification by each party is important at this stage.

Here again the importance of flexibility must be stressed. A negotiator must be ready to reevaluate her goals, reservation price, and BATNA throughout the negotiations, based upon altered perceptions and acquisition of new information. For example, if one goes into an employment negotiation with a particular understanding of the job description and determines during the negotiation that the job description is different than initially believed, such information could alter goals, reservation price (or salary), and BATNA. If, during the course of a negotiation over the rental of an apartment, the landlord learns that the tenant, who is a second-year graduate student, also has a permanent teaching position at the university, the landlord may alter his perception of the longevity of the leasehold, which can affect other issues being discussed.

Timing is also very important. A good negotiator is patient and sensitive to the other party's sense of time.

> [T]he bargainer who is willing to wait longer, to probe more patiently, to appear less eager for a settlement will be more successful. . . . Many Americans are uncomfortable with long pauses in the give-and-take of negotiations. They feel obliged to say something, anything, to get the negotiations rolling. However, it's not what is

---

12 Singer, *supra* note 5, at 18.

said in negotiations that counts, but what isn't said. Very often the strategic essence of a negotiation exercise is merely a waiting game with self-imposed penalties (embarrassment) for delays.[13]

Closing of Negotiations

At the end of the negotiation, parties should be in a position to make commitments. If total agreement cannot be reached in one session, affirm those issues that have been agreed upon and establish other meeting dates and times. If all issues are resolved, confirm the resolution in writing, if appropriate, review it to make sure all parties understand and are satisfied, confirm that there are no other outstanding issues, and end the meeting. Parties may want counsel to review any binding contract prior to signing. If no agreement can be reached, end the meeting, but leave the door open for future negotiations. Such future negotiations might include introducing an intervenor or broadening the issues being negotiated.

Other Factors

These steps in the process of negotiation will be affected by the number and complexity of issues, the number of parties involved, whether the parties are present, whether there are party representatives, the experience the negotiators and/or the parties have with each other, the custom of the area (both geographical and professional), and the culture of the parties.

Complex issues, numerous issues, and/or numerous parties will generally require more than one negotiation session. However, "[b]ecause of the possibilities for trade-offs, multi-issue disputes often turn out to be easier to resolve than single issues, which may allow less room for creative swaps."[14] As for multi-party disputes, "there is [also] a vast difference between conflicts involving two disputants and those involving more than two disputants. Once three or more conflicting parties are involved, coalitions of disputants may form and may act in concert against the other disputants."[15] To put it differently, "[i]f you decide not to come to an agreement with all of your adversaries, you might still forge an agreement with a subset of the other parties. In other words, you can still cooperate with a coalition of some of the others. If there is only one other party, this complexity can't be formulated."[16]

---

13 Raiffa, *supra* note 6, at 78.

14 Singer, *supra* note 5, at 8.

15 Raiffa, *supra* note 6, at 11.

16 *Id.* at 252.

Representatives of a party who is not present at the negotiation, such as attorneys or ambassadors, will need to confirm any agreement reached at the negotiation with their client. When a party comprises a group of people, there may be conflict within that group as to the desired outcome and a negotiator will have to deal with those conflicts and reach a consensus regarding participation in any agreement.

If the parties or their representatives are accustomed to dealing with each other, such as in labor negotiations, there will be certain customs and relationships that have built up over the years that will affect negotiations. Finally, the custom of the business or profession — e.g., diplomats, agency representatives, realtors, environmentalists, builders, landlords — as well as the custom of the area — e.g., northeast vs. southwest United States, North American vs. Japanese — will affect the formalities and structure of the process.

Other peripherals that can affect negotiating include "differences in initial endowments or wealth, differences in time-related costs, differences in perceived determination or aggressiveness, differences in marginal valuations, differences in needs, and differences in the number of people comprising each side."[17]

Enforceability of a negotiated agreement can be an issue. We generally consider a negotiated agreement a contract, which is enforceable in a civil suit. Sometimes, such a settlement is made part of a court judgment and enforceable as such.

However, consider an international agreement, in which there is no enforcement mechanism, no international court to force compliance. Scholars of this subject have determined that "[t]he best way to secure a contract, when there are no binding, legal, enforcement mechanisms, is through the linkages of continuing involvement."[18] For example, consider a major power that wants to set up oil drilling in a small country but is concerned that once the drilling is established, the small country will force it to leave and will take over the operation. What authority could the major country go to for enforcement of the original agreement? In this case, the major power could allay its concerns by linking the successful operation of the drilling sites to continuing preferred trading status to the minor nation. Such status would be too beneficial to the smaller nation to jeopardize by taking over the drilling sites. Obviously, linkages can be made in domestic situations as well.

Summary

Negotiation takes place in stages and each stage contains several steps. There are three basic stages to each negotiation: preliminary discussions, the central part of the negotiation, and the closing. Negotiations are affected by the number of parties and

---

17 *Id.* at 54.

18 *Id.* at 198.

issues, the presence of representatives, differing cultures, and the enforceability of the contract, among others. In preparing for or studying a negotiation, one should consider the following:

1. How many parties are involved?

2. If a party consists of a group, are they united in their goals?

3. Will these parties or these negotiators face each other again in the future?

4. Can the current issues be linked to future contacts?

5. How many issues are there?

6. Is an agreement required by law, as for public employees?

7. Are the parties to the dispute present at the negotiating table, or is ratification required?

8. Should a competitive or cooperative approach be utilized?

9. Are there time constraints or time-related costs?

10. Are the contracts binding?

11. Are the negotiations private or public?

12. What are the group norms: cooperative? competitive? in-between?

13. Is third-party intervention possible or appropriate?[19]

14. What is the authority of a representative negotiator?

Communication Skills

Verbal Communication

The most important communication skill in the negotiation process is the ability to express an idea or concept in a way that the others will hear and understand what you say. That requires clarity and directness. It may also require the use of nonattacking language. For example, in negotiating the purchase of a car, the skilled buyer might say, "I hear you saying that you believe the car is actually worth $1,200. I don't agree with you; but let's look at the 'blue book' value or at advertisements for similar cars in the newspaper. It's not that I undervalue your car, I can really only afford to pay $800."

---

19 *Id.* at 11-19.

A more confrontational buyer, on the other hand, might say, "That car isn't worth $500.00, much less $1,200! How stupid can you be? (or do you think I am?) I wouldn't pay more than _____ for that piece of junk!" The person selling the car is much more likely to respond positively to the first communication rather than the second. Why? It focuses on the issue at hand, not the people, and it utilizes outside standards or criteria as a basis for setting value.

How can this expressive ability be developed? One way is to practice. Part of collaborative communication is to address the issue, not attack the other negotiator. One can honestly disagree as to the value of a car, but calling the other person names or disparaging her property or her position accomplishes little. One way to practice this skill is to speak with someone with whom you disagree on a particular issue. See if you can express your point of view in a nonthreatening and respectful manner. After the other side also expresses her ideas, reword her position as a way of communicating that you understand that position. This latter skill reflects the second most important communication skill — active listening and the ability to reword and repeat what someone else has said.

Listening Skills

Active, concentrated listening is essential. A person cannot effectively listen if her mind is elsewhere, thinking, for example, about what she is going to say when the speaker is finished talking. Most people cannot listen effectively if they are enraged by what the other person has said or done. An individual must concentrate on the matter at hand: She must listen, take time to reflect, and then either respond or rephrase what she hears the other person has said. This approach has two benefits, it helps the listener understand the other person's position better and it conveys to the speaker that you have been listening to them. Consider how frustrating it is to speak to someone who is not listening to you!

The following checklists can serve as guidelines for improving listening skills.

Active Listening Skills

1.   Maintain eye contact.

2.   Make appropriate verbal responses to what the speaker says.

3.   Pay attention. Don't let your mind wander to something else or to what you are going to say when the other person stops talking.

4.   Maintain attentive body language.

5.   Stop doing other things.

6. Avoid distractions, i.e., TV, computer, others talking.

7. Listen for feelings.

8. Encourage "I" messages.

Reflective Listening Skills

1. Restate what the other person has said, and obtain their affirmation that your understanding is accurate.

2. Restate what the other person has said in nonjudgmental language.

3. Ask the speaker to clarify what they have said.

4. Keep your demeanor and tone of voice calm.

5. Be interested.

6. Summarize what the person has said.

Nonverbal Communication

Communication is more than just the use of words. It comprises all the ways in which someone has an impact on another person. Nonverbal communication includes the volume, rate, and pitch of one's voice, as well as body language and facial expressions. For example, while we might like to believe that our pets understand the words we use, it is more likely that they respond to the manner in which we say things. Try saying to a dog in an authoritative manner, "Tasha, go lay down." Then say "Tasha, go eat your dinner" in the same tone of voice, with the same inflection. She will probably react in the same way; that is, she will respond as if she is being disciplined. Repeat both statements in a loving, kind, and encouraging voice and she will respond to those statements as if she were being praised. Similarly, a person's response to some communication is influenced, and sometimes determined, by the manner in which it is communicated. The great orator Dr. Martin Luther King Jr. captured his listeners' attention through his presentation, as well as his words.

Other Issues

People react or respond differently to a speaker who speaks loudly, with medium volume, or quietly. Someone who has some difficulty hearing may prefer a loud speaker. A quiet person may prefer a quiet speaker. A speaker should control the volume of his speech so that others can comfortably hear without being overly loud. The rate of one's speech also bears attention. If a listener herself is a rapid speaker and is listening to a slower speaker, she might be tempted to finish sentences for the slower speaker. This can be very annoying and can result in miscommunication. Respect for other people's pace is an integral part of good communication. A speaker must also be aware of the pitch (high, medium, or low) of his voice and its impact on others.

The speaker needs to be sensitive to these things in himself and in others to be an effective communicator. A good negotiator is aware of the spoken language he uses as well as the power of his nonverbal communication. He is also aware of these in others and his reaction to them. Have you ever wondered why some people really "get on your nerves," even though they have said or done nothing to justify your annoyance? Perhaps the manner in which they communicate reminds you of someone you dislike. In negotiating with such a person, you would have to be aware of your reaction and guard against its influencing your ability to effectively communicate and negotiate. Culture also affects communication. In addition to the above items, the density of language used as well as physical proximity affect communication. For example, in some cultures speakers stand closer to their listeners, which can cause discomfort and inattention in a listener from a different culture.

Applications

Professional Fulfillment

While the skills involved in negotiation have broad life applications, the purpose here is to focus on workplace applications. First is the area of professional self-improvement. In the workplace, one negotiates for promotions, raises, benefits, particular work assignments, continuing education, and professional opportunities.

Consider the following situation: A paralegal, who has worked in a medium-sized law firm for approximately two years, wants to attend continuing education seminars periodically and wants the firm to pay for these seminars and give him time off to attend them. First the preparation: he should determine what the firm policy has been previously with regard to continuing education opportunities, for attorneys as well as paralegals; determine how other similarly sized firms treat the issue; approximate the cost to the firm in dollars and lost time; and approximate the benefit to the firm in expanded knowledge and improved morale. He should consider approaching others in the firm regarding who in authority should be asked about this issue and how they should be approached.

Next, the paralegal must practice the negotiation several times with a friend and then make an appointment with the individual in the firm who makes these personnel decisions. When commencing the negotiation, he will present his best position and try to obtain from the other person their underlying interests. How can both parties have their needs met within the framework of the firm and its resources? He should ask the other person what she suggests be done to resolve the issue. Encourage brainstorming. Remember, it is the problem that must be solved, not the parties who should be attacked. The paralegal must demonstrate to the manager or partner that he is sensitive to her issues as well as his own, but is firm in attempting to satisfying his needs. If the attorney or manager reacts in an unpleasant way, he should leave the door open for future negotiations. If a resolution cannot be reached, he will try to make sure there is an opportunity for further discussions.

On Behalf of the Employer

Another negotiating opportunity exists in the workplace in dealing with vendors of products and services for the firm or company. For example, one may be asked to determine which litigation software is best suited for the firm, corporation, or agency and then negotiate with the vendor regarding installation, training, and support. An office manager may engage the services of a temporary personnel agency and negotiate the terms of the relationship on behalf of the employer.

Rulemaking Negotiation

Many people think of negotiating in terms of resolving an existing conflict. However, negotiation and mediation are becoming tools for developing legislation and making rules for broad promulgation. An individual working with a legislator or an agency (state or federal) that develops and proposes legislation and/or rules may be involved in such rulemaking negotiation with parties who have conflicting interests in the proposed legislation or rules. This process is called "negotiated rulemaking" or "reg-neg." This process has been used at the federal level by the Environmental Protection Agency, the Department of Education, the Department of Housing and Urban Development, and the Occupational Safety and Health Administration, among others, as well as on the state level.

Ethics

Ethical Rules

Attorney negotiators are bound by the American Bar Association's Rules of Professional Conduct[20] as adopted by the state in which they practice. These rules

---

20   Model Rules of Professional Conduct 4.1(a), 4.2(a) (2002).

require honesty, professionalism, and fair dealing. Paralegals who work with attorneys are agents of the attorneys and must comply with the same rules.[21] In addition, both the National Federation of Paralegal Associations (NFPA) and the National Association of Legal Assistants (NALA) have promulgated, or put into effect, rules regarding the behavior of paralegals. The American Arbitration Association, the American Bar Association, and the Society of Professionals in Dispute Resolution (now the Association for Conflict Resolution) developed Model Standards of Conduct for Mediators (see Appendix A).

Attorneys have no affirmative duty to inform others of relevant facts. It is the responsibility of both sides to do their own research, factual investigation, and discovery. An attorney cannot expect his adversary to do his work for him.

Representative Conflict

A concern for attorney or other agent negotiators is the potential conflict between their own personal and professional interests and those of the client in negotiating a settlement. In avoiding litigation by negotiating a settlement that is satisfactory to the client, the attorney is potentially reducing her own fee, whether it is on an hourly basis or is a contingency fee. Of primary importance is the rule that all settlement offers must be communicated to the client and the client must ultimately decide whether or not to accept the offer (Model Rules of Professional Conduct 1.2(a), and 1.4). Such a decision is often made with the advice of counsel; but just as litigation is authorized by the client, so is the settlement. In providing advice to the client, the attorney must be aware of her own self-interests and not let those interests interfere with the client's decision.

Other potential scenarios of conflict include an attorney who is intent on searching for an objectively fair and impartial outcome and a client who simply wants the best possible outcome for himself. Or consider the potential conflict between a client who, because of a valuable long-term relationship, wants to maintain good relations with the other side, but is represented by someone who is out to get the most for his client and thereby enhance his reputation as a "killer."[22]

"Differing goals and standards of agent and principal may create conflicting pulls. For example, the buyer's agent may be compensated as a percentage of the purchase price, thus creating an incentive to have the price as high as possible. The buyer, of course, wants the lowest possible price."[23]

---

21 NALA Canon 6 (2004).

22 Stephen B. Goldberg et al., Dispute Resolution: Negotiation, Mediation, and Other Processes 5th ed. 67 (2007).

23 *Id.* at 67.

Truth

One walks a fine line between negotiating aggressively on behalf of oneself or another and not misrepresenting or lying about the issues. Exaggeration or "puffing" is permitted, but factual misrepresentation is not. In negotiating the sale and purchase of an automobile, for example, the parties can exaggerate or understate what they believe the value of the car to be; but neither party should misrepresent such matters as whether the car has been involved in an accident or one's ability to pay. Consider the case in which the seller of an auto represented to the purchaser that he was selling it for a friend and that it had not been in an accident. The purchaser bought the car and subsequently found out that the seller was selling it for a dealership and that it had been in an accident and the frame had been damaged. The seller was guilty of fraud in this case.

The role that truth plays in negotiation will depend on the parties, the environment, and the issues. A certain degree of exaggeration is acceptable in some situations and frowned upon in others.

> The art of compromise centers on the willingness to give up something in order to get something else in return. Successful artists get more than they give up. A common ploy is to exaggerate the importance of what one is giving up and to minimize the importance of what one gets in return. Such posturing is part of the game. In most cultures these self-serving negotiating stances are expected, as long as they are kept in decent bounds. [However,] strategic misrepresentation can cause inefficiencies. Consider a distributive bargaining problem in which there is a zone of agreement in actual, but not necessarily in revealed, reservation prices. An inefficiency can arise only if the parties fail to come to an agreement. By bargaining hard the parties may fail to come to an agreement even though any point in the zone of agreement would yield a better outcome for both than the no-agreement state. Still, one cannot conclude from this observation that a negotiator should unilaterally and truthfully reveal his or her reservation price.... [N]egotiators [should] act openly and honestly on efficiency concerns; tradeoffs should be disclosed (if the adversary reciprocates), but reservation prices should be kept private.... [E]ach negotiator is well advised to behave cooperatively and honestly (for example, by disclosing trade-offs) in seeking joint gains, but to bargain more toughly when it comes to sharing the jointly created pie.[24]

---

24   Raiffa, *supra* note 6, at 142-144.

A Higher Standard

Extreme competitiveness, while a potent tool, can also create ethical conflicts for the negotiator. Consider the following:

> Imagine that you have to choose whether to act nobly or selfishly. If you act nobly you will be helping others at your own expense; if you act selfishly you will be helping yourself at others' expense. Similarly, those others have similar choices. In order to highlight the tension between helping yourself and helping others, let's specify that if all participants act nobly, all do well and the society flourishes; but regardless of how others act, you can always do better for yourself, as measured in tangible rewards (say, profits), if you act selfishly — but at the expense of others. Leaving morality aside for the moment, the best tangible reward accrues to you in this asocial game if you act selfishly and all others act nobly. But if all behave that way, all suffer greatly.[25]

Another reason mitigating against dishonesty or like behavior is that it harms the reputation of the negotiator in the long run.

The point to be made here is that negotiators must always be conscious of ethical considerations, must continually look at their behavior in light of such ethics, and must be aware of the well-being of others and of long-term societal interests. If one does so, he might set an example that can positively influence the behavior of others.

Confidentiality

Confidentiality needs to be considered in two different contexts. The first is that whenever a paralegal is present during a negotiation or, while serving as an advocate, negotiates on behalf of a client, the requirement of confidentiality prohibits the paralegal from discussing the client's affairs with others not involved in the negotiation. A paralegal cannot participate in a negotiation session and then go home and tell his spouse or friends about the negotiation. This is a violation of both the attorney's Code of Professional Responsibility and NALA Canon 7.

The second context is litigation. Any negotiations that qualify as settlement discussions cannot be disclosed during trial and are not subject to discovery.

---

25 *Id.* at 346.

EXERCISES

1. Plan an actual negotiation. Keep a record of all the steps in which you engage during the entire process. Prepare; practice; do the negotiation. Evaluate your performance and evaluate the other party's performance.

2. Observe a negotiation, either in person or on videotape, and (1) identify the steps in the process and (2) determine whether or not there were any ethical problems for the negotiators.

3. Do an introspective inventory to determine what type of negotiator you are.

4. Recall something you said recently that made another person angry, and reword what you said so that it would be less likely to cause the same response.

5. Talk with an attorney about negotiation and make a list of the professional negotiations in which the attorney engages.

6. Research rules and statutes in your state regarding the requirement of good faith efforts to settle litigation. Do the same research for case law.

7. Research the issue of confidentiality of settlement negotiations in your jurisdiction.

Negotiation Role Plays

A Family in Crisis (three parties)

Steve and Donna Stone have a daughter, Sara, and a younger son, Mark. Sara is attending her first year at a public college, located about 150 miles from their home. While tuition is reasonable, the parents, who are separated, are struggling to pay Sara's tuition and room and board. They discover by accident that she is not attending class regularly and is, therefore, doing very poorly in most of her classes. They confront her with this information and a heated conflict ensues, with Sara accusing her parents of violating her privacy and caring more about money than her. The parents, while normally not in agreement these days, join in accusing Sara of wasting their money and her time. After this confrontation, they go their separate ways. The next weekend Sara is due to come home and her parents want to have a further discussion regarding this issue. Sara has generally been able to talk with her parents and wants to continue in college. Therefore, it is in her best interest to talk with her parents and try to explain her situation.

Office Injustices (five parties)

You are part of a paralegal litigation team. There are three attorneys presently working on a substantial civil matter, which is scheduled for arbitration in six months. First on the team is George Hathaway, the lead attorney who will be taking the matter to arbitration. He is considered a good lawyer and a good litigator, but is distant and a workaholic. The second attorney is Susan McDonald, a mature expert in environmental litigation. She is a hard worker, though not as driven as Hathaway. The third member of the litigation team, Rodney Long, is a legal scholar who is a little out of place with the two aggressive litigators. He is respected for his knowledge, but not for his commitment to ADR, which he is constantly urging everyone to consider.

The paralegals on the team are Larry Lomax, Stephanie Strong, Sheila Thompson, and Lorraine Li. Lorraine is the lead paralegal and has been with the firm for many years. She is knowledgeable and hardworking. She sometimes takes abuse from the attorneys and passes it on to the paralegals. She is in charge of work assignments, while also responsible for her own paralegal work. Sheila Thompson appears to be a weak link in the team. She was just hired and is very inexperienced. Her attendance is also a problem and it takes her too long to get the work done. However, the attorneys like her because she is very personable and knows how to stroke their egos. Stephanie has been at the firm for about a year and is a certified paralegal. She is very career-oriented and is a good contributor to the team, but her interpersonal skills are sometimes lacking. Finally, Larry is Mr. Nice Guy. He works hard, but his major asset is his ability to get along with everyone. He is the first African-American in this law firm.

Recently, several issues have arisen to cause dissension on the team: work distribution, overtime, and professional development, i.e., the firm's support of continuing education for the paralegals through payment of tuition, fees for continuing education courses, time off to attend seminars, or professional conferences. Lorraine has responsibility for work distribution, but George Hathaway is the authority on the other matters. Rodney has noticed a morale problem among the paralegals and has suggested a meeting of the team to resolve some of the problems.

The Computer System (two parties)

The law firm of Long, Tyrol & Kamp is located in the suburbs of Denver, Colorado. They are a relatively young firm that has become well known for their representation of gay activists, fighting for gay employment and health rights. Now others battling discriminatory treatment are beginning to come to them for help and their business is improving.

Jerry Tyne is the paralegal. He has been with the firm almost since its inception and is highly regarded by the three attorneys who make up the firm. He is computer knowledgeable and has been urging the firm to upgrade their computer system, which will benefit both the attorneys and him. Pat Long, one of the partners, has resisted, probably because she is "computer phobic." However, the other partners and Jerry have finally convinced her. They have assigned Jerry the responsibility of finding the appropriate software and hardware within a given budget. Jerry is thrilled. He puts together an outline of what he believes the firm needs: word processing, electronic mail, docket control, litigation system, deposition reading system, spreadsheet program, communications system, and networking. He contacts a number of firms and gets proposals from each. He has narrowed it down to one company, and is now negotiating price and services.

The company, Compros, will provide five computers, and Microsoft Office 2007™ for word processing and spread sheets, e-mail capability, a docket control package, a litigation system, and a deposition reading system. (Jerry would like to see the firm get a subscription to Lexis™ or Westlaw™.) Compros will network the computers to facilitate information sharing.

The Japanese Businessman(two parties)

The law firm of Carnival, Struts, Styne, and Taylor has begun to expand into the international business arena. Jason Carnival has been serving as an arbitrator in several international business disputes, particularly involving European and Asian transactions. As a result, his reputation in these communities has grown and he recently received an inquiry from a Japanese manufacturing company regarding representation in the United States. After a number of delays and a great deal of "telephone tag," he arranged an appointment with Charles Liu, an attorney from Japan, who represented the company in its country of origin. Mr. Carnival was very excited about the prospect of cultivating this contact with an eye to future legal business.

The appointment was scheduled for last Monday at 10:00 A.M. In anticipation of the meeting, Mr. Carnival spent the week reading whatever he could get his hands on regarding the Japanese business and legal culture. In addition, he spoke to several other attorneys who had experience with Japanese businessmen. He researched the specific company and spent some time on the Internet to further expand his knowledge of the ways in which American and Japanese businessmen and attorneys are similar in their approach to a business meeting and how they differ. Needless to say, he was as prepared as he could be. His paralegal, Joyce Summers, had done some of the research for him and had summarized her findings. She knew how concerned he was that this meeting proceed to establish a long-term arrangement.

The Thursday before the meeting, Mr. Carnival had to fly to Chicago for depositions, which lasted through Friday and Saturday morning. He was scheduled to fly back to Los Angeles on Sunday morning. There was a blizzard in the Midwest on Sunday and no flights were permitted to leave. The airlines were, however, promising that service would be returning to normal at midnight. Therefore, although he was concerned, Mr. Carnival rescheduled his return flight for 1:00 A.M. on Monday.

Meanwhile, back at Carnival, Struts, Styne, and Taylor, the flu was raging through the office personnel. Both his secretary and his paralegal, Ms. Summers, fell ill and were bedridden. By Monday morning there was only a skeleton crew at the law firm. Worse yet, there was a total breakdown of communications; messages left by Mr. Carnival on the receptionist's voice mail, as well as that of his secretary and partners, went unheard. Present in the office at 10:00 A.M. were Joshua Lopez, an associate; Robyn Rosen, Mr. Struts's secretary; Greg Wozniak, a recently hired paralegal; and someone from the word processing department. Ms. Rosen was sitting at the receptionist's desk, frustrated because she was unable to accomplish her own work while answering telephones and dealing with visitors.

When Mr. Liu arrived, Ms. Rosen began a search for Mr. Carnival and finally determined, after about half an hour, that he was still stuck in Chicago. Mr. Liu explained that he was scheduled to fly back to Japan that afternoon and could he at least meet with someone. Ms. Rosen spoke with Mr. Lopez, but he was working on an Order to Show Cause that was scheduled before the judge at 1:00 that afternoon. Lopez apologized, but indicated that it would be impossible to meet with Mr. Liu. Next, Ms. Rosen called Mr. Wozniak to meet with Mr. Liu and they met in his office for about half an hour. After that Mr. Liu left and Mr. Wozniak returned to his work.

On Tuesday morning, when things began to return to normal and Mr. Carnival was able to get a flight home, he called Mr. Wozniak and thanked him for helping out and asked what had been discussed at the meeting. Mr. Wozniak said he had apologized for Mr. Carnival's inadvertent cancellation and that the meeting had been strained, but that Mr. Liu had asked a number of personal questions, followed by some questions about the firm and then left. When Mr. Carnival arrived in the office, he called Mr. Liu in Japan and was told he was not in and would not be available for some time. Mr. Carnival began to get an uneasy feeling, but other work demanded his attention. When he did not receive a return call by Thursday, he called again and was told the same thing. He decided to write to Mr. Liu and also to sit down with Mr. Wozniak, explain some of the things he had learned about the Japanese culture and way of doing business, and find out more specifically what had transpired at the meeting.

Mediation

Facilitative Skills
> Communication Skills
> Interpersonal Skills

Neutrality
> What Is It?
> Power Imbalances

Applications
> Community Disputes
> School Mediation
> Criminal Mediation
> Mediation of Civil Matters
> Mediation of Family Matters
> Mediation of Administrative Matters
> Labor Relations
> Construction Mediation
> Environmental Mediation
> Commercial Mediation
> International Mediation

Ethics
> Self-Determination
> Impartiality
> Confidentiality
> Conflicts of Interest
> Competence
> Illegal Agreements
> Appropriate Parties and Unrepresented Interests
> Power Imbalances
> Language
> Disclosure of Criminal Activity

Summary

Exercises

Mediation Role Plays
> Neighborhood Dispute (four individuals, two parties)
> Women in College (two mediators, six parties)
> Corporate Legal Department (two parties)

Introduction

Mediation is practiced in many forms and in a variety of settings. It is rapidly becoming embedded in our legal system. It is a mode of dispute resolution that introduces a third-party neutral, or neutrals (co-mediation), to assist the disputing parties in addressing their conflict.

> The process utilizes a neutral third party . . . to facilitate communication between the disputants, to assist them in defining the issues in dispute, to help them develop options and alternatives, and to reach a consensual resolution that is satisfactory and agreeable to all involved.[1]

Participation by the disputants in mediation is generally voluntary, although in court connected mediation there is sometimes a mandatory orientation meeting to introduce the parties to the process. Occasionally, participation in the entire process is mandated either by contract or by the court. In the latter situation, however, the disputants cannot be forced to reach agreement. The neutral mediator cannot impose a decision on the parties the way an arbitrator or judge does. Rather, the mediator uses a wide range of skills to facilitate communication among the parties looking toward a better understanding of each other's position, a recognition of their own interests, and a resolution of their conflict. "The mediator is a conflict manager and resolution facilitator."[2]

Mediation has been called "facilitated negotiation." It can be a very exciting process for all the parties because it requires disputant participation and an expansion of understanding and communication skills. The parties or disputants are encouraged to be in control of the process, rather than giving up control to a decisionmaker. It is informal and can be less threatening than a court proceeding and permits the parties to express their feelings, to improve their own communication skills, and to hear the other side of the conflict. This setting, combined with the skills of the mediator and the parties' desire to end the conflict, helps to bring the disputants into an agreement that resolves their conflict. It is not surprising, therefore, that studies indicate that a mediated agreement is more likely to be complied with than a judgment imposed by a judge or arbitrator.

For mediation to be successful, disputants sometimes have to alter their perspective. In the United States, we are a very competitive people and place a high

---

1 Samuel G. Forlenza, Mediation and Psychotherapy: Parallel Processes, *in* Community Mediation: A Handbook for Practitioners and Researchers 228 (Karen Duffy et al. eds., 1991) (citations omitted).

2 *Id.* at 230.

premium on "winning." In approaching mediation, "[t]he important consideration is not who is 'right' and therefore 'wins' but rather what is the solution that meets the needs of the problem and with which the disputants can live."[3]

In a mediation, the parties, and sometimes their representatives, meet with the mediator(s) to discuss the dispute. Each participant has an opportunity to "tell his or her side of the story." The parties are told to be respectful, to listen attentively, to not interrupt each other, and to not engage in other openly hostile behavior, such as name-calling. If the mediator thinks it appropriate, she can meet with each party individually (caucus) to examine that party's interests and positions and to better understand each side of the conflict. Disputants also sometimes find it easier to speak privately to a neutral and are willing to let the neutral speak on their behalf to the other parties in order to communicate their desires. However, no information obtained in the caucus can be communicated to the other party without permission of the individual with whom she caucused.

Through this process of direct and indirect communication, the parties come to a better understanding of their own needs, the other parties' needs, and the value of creating their own solution. The parties, through this better understanding of their own needs and interests, may become more empowered to express those needs productively in the joint session. This ultimately brings them closer to a solution.

Preparation for Mediation

Mediator Preparation

There are many instances where the mediator has no knowledge of the facts or circumstances of the conflict prior to meeting with the parties. In those situations, the mediator is obviously unable to do any factual preparation. However, a good mediator will at least prepare and practice an introduction/opening statement and provide a comfortable, nonthreatening environment for the mediation.

In business mediation, particularly through the American Arbitration Association, the parties can submit a Request for Mediation to open a case. The mediator will read all material submitted by the parties prior to the first meeting.

In some mediation practices, the parties have met with someone from the mediation center as part of the intake process prior to formal mediation. This can result in the mediator commencing the mediation session with a greater knowledge of the

---

3 Andrea Nager Chasen, Defining Mediation and Its Use for Paralegals, 9. J. Paralegal Edu. & Prac. 64 (1993).

dispute. Whatever degree of information the mediator has available to him, he should familiarize himself with it prior to the mediation session.

It should be noted, however, that there is a difference of opinion in the field as to whether the mediator should be familiar with the facts and positions of the parties prior to mediation. Some believe that when the mediator possesses such information, she can expedite the mediation and minimize the parties' getting entrenched when stating their positions. Others believe that the mediator should go into the mediation with a clean slate and without any preconceived ideas based on submissions by the parties. Further, these theorists argue that when parties prepare pre-mediation filings, they become committed to particular positions and are less amenable to looking at interests underlying those positions and thereby working toward resolution.

Party Preparation

The parties prepare for a mediation in the same way they prepare for a negotiation. (See Chapter 3, at pages 43-46.) They critically analyze and evaluate their own issues, as well as obtain all possible information about other disputants' issues. They consider their best alternative to a negotiated agreement (BATNA).[4] They determine their optimum and least desirable, but acceptable, result. In so doing, they produce a range in which settlement is acceptable to them. They may role-play and brainstorm creative ways to address their conflict. At a minimum, the parties can prepare their own written positions, so that when they have the opportunity to speak at the mediation, they can be clear and precise and not omit any important issues. Such a written preparation can also aid in overcoming nervousness at the mediation. They may also wish to prepare a draft agreement for use in the mediation.

Methodology

The role of the mediator is the major differentiating factor in the following mediation models.

There is a continuum of roles, from weak to strong, that a mediator can play. On the weak side, the mediator may be just a convener of meetings or a nonsubstantive, neutral discussion leader; he or she might simply maintain rules of civilized debate or occasionally give a reticent speaker a chance to interject some comments.[5]

---

4   See Roger Fisher et al., Getting to Yes 99, 100 (2d ed. 1991). See also Chapter 3, infra.

5   Howard Raiffa, The Art & Science of Negotiation 218 (1982). Reprinted 2005.

On the stronger side of the continuum, mediators are more participatory and suggest solutions and urge agreement. A great deal of this difference has to do with mediator directiveness, from very directive to very nondirective.[6]

Facilitative Model

In the facilitative model, the mediator is a manager of communication and does very little to suggest resolutions to the parties. He encourages brainstorming, reality testing, and increased communication among the parties to bring them to their own settlement. The benefit of this model is that it permits the exploration and expression of emotions and the parties are better able to develop their own solution. This process, however, can be time-consuming and thus may be inappropriate in a setting where time constraints are an issue.

Proponents of this model strongly favor the nondirective mediator role as providing the better chance at reaching a lasting resolution of the dispute. "Although research on mediation styles is in its infancy, there is some evidence that the more active or controlling mediators achieve higher rates of settlement, but that these agreements are more likely to collapse over time."[7]

Evaluative Model

Another type of mediation, more likely to be used in business or commercial disputes, is one in which the mediator is a more active participant in evaluating the conflict, suggesting resolutions, and urging acceptance of resolutions. Here, the mediator's knowledge of the subject matter of the dispute is valuable. Consider a dispute over construction issues, for example, where the disputants are both business people and want a neutral who will be informed, be able to understand their conflict, and actively assist them in their discussions, debates, and, ultimately, their creation of an agreement. Frequently, more complex and controversial issues mandate that the mediators will become actively involved.

The parties are likely more concerned with the efficiency of the process and the knowledge of the mediator than in expression of emotions.

---

6 For an excellent exposition on this topic, see Christoher W. Moor, The Mediation Process, 43-56 (3rd ed. 2003).

7 Linda R. Singer, Settling Disputes: Conflict Resolution in Business, Families, and The Legal System 40 (2d ed. 1994).

Single-Text Mediation

Utilizing a single text (see single text negotiation in Chapter 3) is a mediation method that focuses on one proffered resolution or agreement, which the parties modify until they are satisfied. In this way, the parties are led to concentrate on the vehicle for solution, not their individual differences. This approach is particularly useful in mediation because "[t]he mediator . . . prepare[s] a single negotiating text and then successively modifies it after the disputants have criticized it separately and collectively. . . ."[8]

Transformative Model

Douglas Yarn, in the Dictionary of Conflict Resolution at page 418, describes transformative mediation as "mediation in which disputants have the opportunity to increase their own capacity to work through their own problems and to understand the perspectives of others." Transformative mediation, developed by Folger and Bush, focuses on changing the conflict relationship through empowerment of self (strengthened self-awareness) and recognition of the other person's situations and human qualities. The focus is not on settlement of a distinct conflict, but rather a transformation of the conflict relationship between the parties, and ultimately the larger community.[9]

Therapy/Counseling vs. Mediation

Traditionally, a distinction is made between mediation and psychotherapy or counseling. Certainly they do share some common attributes, and there is a place for certain therapeutic techniques in the mediation process. However, dispute resolution professionals stress that therapy and mediation are different processes and should not be confused. "The role of counselors often is to facilitate ongoing and in-depth exploration of personal issues, with the goal of dealing with problems rooted in the past. For a mediation to occur, there must be a discrete dispute."[10]

Other Variations

Practitioners will discover that there are many variations on these models, as well as other mediation or conflict resolution paradigms. Co-mediation, for example, utilizes two or more mediators as neutrals. This provides greater ability of the mediator to hear, see, and understand what is occurring in the mediation, as well as the opportunity for

---

8   Raiffa, *supra* note 5, at 220.

9   Robert A. Baruch Bush and Joseph P. Folger. The Promise of Mediation. 2005.

10 Selma Myers & Barbara Filner, Mediation Across Cultures — A Handbook About Conflict and Culture 20 (1994) (citations omitted).

the disputants to gain the expertise of more than one mediator (attorney and mental health professional, for example). The difficulty of co-mediation can be the cost and the possibility of disagreement between the mediators.

A mediator needs to be sensitive to the needs of the parties and the organizational structure in which she works to determine which mediation model is best suited for each case. Some parties will be unable to function within the framework of the existing model of mediation; therefore, mediation will fail if the mediator is insensitive to this issue or unable to fashion a more acceptable and responsive model. Some sponsoring organizations will permit flexibility and others will not.

It should be noted here that one of the goals of most mediations is an agreement between the parties. Obviously, this is not always attained, although a significant number of mediated cases do result in settlement. Even among those that do not settle, however, the parties generally walk away with an appreciation of the mediation process and a better understanding of their conflict, and may even reach agreement on their own at a later date.

Essential Steps in the Process

One must first understand that mediation, like negotiation, can involve a single issue or multiple issues, two parties or multiple parties. The process can be completed in as little as half an hour, or it can extend over a year or more, with periodic and lengthy meetings. The subject matter can be a neighborhood dispute over a barking dog, or it can comprise a large environmental dispute with the logging industry, the environmentalists, and the community each having a different vested interest in the resolution. Mediation is also useful in addressing international conflicts.[11] Mediation can be mandated by a contract between the parties, be required as a precondition for litigation, be strongly recommended by others, or be voluntarily agreed upon by the parties. Mediation services are provided by individuals in private mediation practice, through dispute resolution organizations, such as Endispute and the American Arbitration Association, through community or school organizations, or under the auspices of the courts. Individuals providing mediation services can be professionally trained and educated mediators, people educated in other professions and trained as mediators, or laypeople trained as mediators. Laypeople will find opportunities to mediate in community justice centers, some municipal courts, the Better Business Bureau, or within a private mediation practice.

---

11   I. William Zartman and Saadia Towal, International Mediation *in* Leashing the Dogs of War, 437 (Chester A. Crocker, et al. eds., 2007).

Where to locate the beginning of the mediation process is not so easy. In some settings, the first step of initial intake is when information is gathered and filed for the mediator's benefit. The parties may then receive an introductory description of the process. In other situations, intake is the filing of a complaint and answer. In still others, intake is the filing of a request for mediation. However, regardless of these variations as to the initial intake, the mediator is usually not involved in this opening step and we will therefore commence our analysis of the process with the mediator's opening statement.

The following steps describe facilitative mediation.

Mediator Introduction

In an introductory session or orientation, the mediator describes the process and the rules to the parties. The mediator explains her role is not to make any binding determination (her neutrality), and that any resolution reached will be the decision of the parties. She describes confidentiality and its impact on the process and explains that she may want to caucus, or meet privately, with each party during the mediation. A new mediator should keep a checklist of what should be included in the mediator's introduction. (See the checklist at page 74.)

The mediator answers any questions the parties may have and attempts to make them feel comfortable and gain their trust. She will ask the parties to agree to certain behavioral constraints, such as not interrupting each other, not calling each other names, being respectful of each other and the mediator, etc. When the orientation is completed, the mediator should confirm the parties' understanding and that there is no conflict of interest. (See Appendix A: Model Standards of Conduct for Mediators.) Sometimes the parties are asked to sign a contract agreeing to the rules and committing to the process.

Party Statements/Factfinding

The mediation then proceeds to fact gathering. Usually the party that brought the conflict to the mediation is asked to "tell his story" first, with the other individual responding when the "complainant" is finished. This order is not mandatory, however, and the mediator can ask either party to start. Who presents the conflict first can be important, as this person frames the issues and the second party is then positioned to respond to that framing. In a multi-party mediation, each party should have the opportunity to present his issues. If multiple issues are disputed, the mediator and the parties may work out an agenda prioritizing the issues. If the parties are able to communicate in each other's presence, then open discussions can begin regarding the issues.

Issue Clarification and Option Generation

The process of factfinding will generally carry over into this next segment of the mediation, just as issue clarification usually begins when the party statements are given. However, in this third phase of mediation, the parties are guided beyond what has happened in the past and are encouraged to look to the future and their vision of the future. To do so, the mediator keeps the parties focused on the issues in dispute and how to resolve them, not on the prior injustices that brought them to mediation in the first place.

The mediator helps the parties express themselves if necessary. This can be done by repeating what each party says in a nonjudgmental fashion or assisting each in caucus to verbalize her interests. When it appears that an impasse has been reached, the mediator keeps the process going by moving on to another issue, breaking the tension by calling a break or facilitating more creative problem solving.

It is the function of the mediator to create an environment where the parties develop their own suggestions for solutions. This may require the mediator initially to request such suggestions for resolution from the parties and to affirmatively explore any suggestions that are made. In a particularly uninhibited environment, the parties are encouraged to brainstorm, which permits individuals to offer any ideas they may have regarding solutions without fear as to how those ideas would be judged. This encourages the free flow of ideas and opens up the opportunity for creative thinking. Ultimately, the parties are encouraged by the mediator to seek joint gains.

Selecting Alternatives/Decisionmaking

In this step of the process, the mediator does reality testing with all parties and explores nonagreement options. Reality testing directs the parties to look critically at their own positions and decide whether they are being practical in their demands. This is accomplished by the mediator's asking each party questions about the merits of their position. Exploring nonagreement options and determining a party's BATNA (see page 45) are part of reality testing. The parties must determine, as best they are able, what will happen if they do not reach an agreement. Will there be litigation? What will litigation cost—economically, emotionally, and in lost time? What is the risk factor, i.e., is a judge likely to decide in their favor? If the judge does decide in their favor, will they be able to collect the judgment amount? Is there an ongoing relationship with the other party that will be destroyed in litigation?

These techniques can be used either in a joint meeting with all parties present or in caucus. The mediator's skill is in encouraging the parties themselves to explore alternative settlement options, which provides them the opportunity to choose one that can best meet the needs of all parties. Through this process, the parties can reach a tentative agreement.

Clarification

Once the facts are gathered, options generated, and the best alternative selected, the mediator must pause and make sure that the parties understand all the terms of the tentative agreement. Beginning mediators are fearful of this step because it may give the disputants an opportunity to rehash their conflict. However, it is essential that all parties understand and agree to the terms of the resolution. Some mediators ask the parties to state in their own words the terms of the agreement so that the mediator can make it part of the written mediation agreement.

Closing

In the closing, the agreement between the parties is confirmed and sometimes committed to writing. Most solutions should be written and signed by the parties, although in some situations they may first want to consult others, such as their attorneys, before signing a formal agreement. The basics of the agreement should be recorded in some manner, however, to ensure that all parties agree to and understand it. In a court program, the parties will sometimes appear before a judge to finalize their agreement in the form of a judgment or court order. In divorce mediation, the parties' agreement becomes the basis for a separation or divorce agreement. A word of caution here: Some states prohibit the mediator from drafting an agreement in a divorce mediation and require that the parties seek individual counsel to write an agreement. Therefore, one must be aware of the regulations and ethical constraints in various jurisdictions.

Some authorities emphasize the value of emotional closure as well, which can be a ceremonial gesture such as a handshake or sharing a cup of coffee. What is deemed appropriate will depend on the nature of the conflict, the parties, and the setting.

Implementation

If the conflict is a public one, or one of the parties represents a large constituency, the agreement may need acceptance by the public or the constituency. Part of the closing may therefore include the development of a plan for presentation, acceptance, implementation, and monitoring of the agreement. The mediator can also serve the function of publicly articulating the rationale for the agreement. Other agreements may require the mediators to oversee the implementation phase. Regardless of whether the mediator is involved, the manner in which the agreement will be carried out must be clearly stated and understood, with as much detail as possible or necessary. It may require that the parties meet again with the mediator for future communication.[12]

Summary of Essential Steps for Mediators

The following checklist can be a useful guide.

Mediator Introduction

1. Introduce self and qualifications.

2. Explain neutrality.

3. Explain the mediation process, including the caucus.

4. Explain the ground rules, i.e., no interrupting, name-calling, etc.

5. Set the tone and tenor and build trust with parties.

6. Explain role as mediator, i.e., not a decisionmaker.

7. Explain the benefits of mediation and show enthusiasm for process.

8. Seek commitment from disputants to mediate in good faith.

9. Thoroughly explain the concept and applicability of confidentiality (and its exceptions, if any).

10. Ask the disputants if they have any questions.

11. Identify any potential conflicts of interest.

12. Reinforce parties' participation or attendance.

13. Explain who goes first and why.

14. Go over "housekeeping" details.

15. Determine whether there are representatives and establish the degree of their participation.

16. Explain possible need for taking notes.

---

12 For other approaches to the steps of mediation, see Kimberlee K. Kovach, Mediation, Principles, and Practice, (3rd ed 2004).

Party Statements/Factfinding

1. Identify order of speaking.

2. Demonstrate or model good listening skills.

3. Make sure only one person speaks at a time.

4. Make sure parties have relatively equal time to speak.

5. Reword judgmental language used by parties.

6. Assess suitability for mediation.

7. Help parties prioritize issues if appropriate.

8. Summarize each party's statement of facts and acknowledge emotions.

Issue Clarification and Option Generation

1. Ask the parties what each is seeking from the mediation.

2. Reinforce points of agreement and determine points of disagreement.

3. Analyze problem in order to ask effective questions.

4. Engage in reality testing at the appropriate time.

5. Ask effective questions intended to obtain necessary information.

6. Focus parties on issues and away from positions.

7. Use the caucus effectively.

8. Ask the parties to put themselves in the other's shoes.

9. Encourage creative problem solving.

10. Engage in brain storming, if appropriate.

11. Clarify or summarize solutions as they are presented.

Selecting Alternatives/Decisionmaking

1. Suggest use of objective criteria.

2. Stress shared interests.

3. Discuss BATNA (not necessary to use words, but use concept).

4. Do reality testing if appropriate.

5. Encourage principled negotiation.

6. Encourage parties to make suggestions for resolution.

7. Avoid exerting inappropriate pressure to resolve dispute.

8. Avoid giving professional (legal) advice.

Clarification

1. Clarify agreement.

2. Affirm that it is the parties' agreement.

3. Confirm that the parties thoroughly understand all elements of the agreement.

Closing

1. Write agreement (if appropriate).

2. Have parties sign agreement, and give each a copy.

3. Refer parties to counsel (if appropriate).

4. Leave door open for future conflict resolution.

5. Close mediation session comfortably.

Generally

1. Demonstrate knowledge of process.

2. Be interested.

3. Direct the process.

4. Encourage appropriate direct communication between the parties.

5. Use neutral language.

6. Demonstrate calming skills when necessary.

7. Demonstrate patience.

8. Keep parties future-oriented.

9. Permit appropriate venting.

10. Demonstrate sensitivity to which issues need resolution and which do not.

Facilitative Skills

Communication Skills

Well-developed communication skills are essential in negotiation and mediation. Foremost among them is the ability to communicate in a nonjudgmental fashion in order to maintain the appearance of neutrality. This is often difficult for those with legal training, as the tendency is to look at conflicts from a right/wrong, win/lose perspective. As mediators, individuals must keep in mind that they are facilitators, not decisionmakers or advocates. Nonjudgmental communication requires the use of neutral language,[13] as well as neutral nonverbal communication. Unless consciously used as a device to help bring the parties to agreement, the mediator should limit facial expressions and body movements that convey surprise, shock, dismay, disbelief, and similar emotion.

The second most important communication skill is the ability to concentrate and listen attentively to each party. This has a number of beneficial consequences. First, each party to a dispute wants someone to listen to them and hear their side of the story. A mediator should look at each individual as she is speaking, listen to what she is saying, and acknowledge what she has said. Such active listening creates a positive environment and makes the party feel affirmed. Second, if the mediator listens carefully, he may pick up clues as to how the conflict can be settled. The parties know the dispute better than the mediator and probably have thought about how it could be resolved. Listen for the parties' solutions. Third, the mediator serves as a model for an active listener. By demonstrating active listening, the mediator accomplishes this and contributes to each party hearing and understanding the interests of the other.[14] Active listening by the mediator helps develop the trust of the parties in the mediator.

Finally, the mediator must be able to reword what a party has said in a nonjudgmental, nonthreatening fashion. This skill allows the mediator to confirm that she has understood what the party said; and by repeating it, she is making sure that the other party understands it too. Because the mediator repeats the party's statement in a nonjudgmental manner, she can take the "sting" out of it. This tactic is not required with every communication; however, when the parties are not understanding each other, it is a powerful tool.

---

13 See chapter 3.

14 For specific techniques, see chapter 3.

Interpersonal Skills

To aid the parties in reaching an agreement, the mediator leads the parties beyond their stated positions and inquires as to their underlying interests and encourages them to recognize those interests and to verbalize them. The mediator assists the parties in thinking creatively about solutions to their conflict. The mediator may question the parties' positions, inquire about the costs of litigation, and recommend the benefits of mediation and the settlement process. Finally, the mediator gives the parties face-saving methods to enable them to move off of their positions, without losing face in front of the other party.

If the parties are locked in a stalemate, the mediator can help move them to another issue. If the parties keep arguing about past injustices, the mediator can help them focus on the future and the possible solution. If the parties do not produce an agreement, the mediator can leave the door open for future discussions. Finally, the mediator can assist the parties in drafting the agreement that they reach.

A final note on style. The mediator has his or her own well-developed personality. It is not suggested that the mediator change his or her personal style. Rather, the mediator should be aware of how that style affects other people and should be flexible enough to modify it if a situation requires. For example, some mediators have very affable and outgoing personalities and will maintain a very positive, relaxed mediation environment. Others are more quiet, restrained, and observant; they tend to create a more professional atmosphere. If the more outgoing mediator is dealing with two very restrained parties, they may find her approach too intrusive. She needs to be aware of this, be flexible, and try to maintain an atmosphere that is comfortable for the parties involved. On the other hand, a more restrained mediator may seem cold and uninterested to a party who is very outgoing, and she likewise must be aware of this and be willing to modify her approach to create greater comfort for the disputants.

Neutrality

What Is It?

Neutrality in mediation is the ability to moderate between individuals in conflict without demonstrating bias in favor of or against any disputant or their interests. While no one can be completely neutral, it is extremely important to remain as neutral as possible when serving as a mediator. It is not the mediator's position to judge the case, the parties, or their actions, except as to behavior that negatively affects the mediation process. It is the parties' dispute and they will create their own solution, with the mediator's assistance and guidance.

The mediator may find that he dislikes one or both of the parties. It is essential, however, that his demeanor and language remain nonjudgmental. If the mediator finds it impossible to remain neutral and the parties or their conflict engenders very strong feelings or reactions in the mediator, it is best to withdraw as the mediator. This is true even through the mediator is not the decision-maker. To do otherwise would be a disservice to the process and the disputants.

To remain neutral requires constant vigilance on the part of the mediator. "Value systems are filled to overflowing with prejudices, opinions, and pre-conceived ideas. Constant vigilance is required so as to not manipulate disputants to a settlement according to what mediators think it should be."[15]

As indicated in the section on communication skills (page 77), retaining the appearance of neutrality through nonjudgmental communication, both verbal and nonverbal, is vital.

Power Imbalances

A secondary issue in neutrality is dealing effectively with power imbalances between the disputants. It may appear to the mediator that there is a serious power difference between the parties. The first step is to determine whether that is the mediator's perception or whether there is in fact a serious power imbalance between the parties. The meek, quiet person is not always weak. Nor is the loud boisterous person always strong. The second step is to determine whether the power imbalance will adversely affect the mediation.

Some writers in this area believe that a mediator should not attempt to balance the distribution of power between parties because that would influence his neutrality or appearance of neutrality. Others say, however, that some power imbalances can be dealt with by having the parties consult counsel or other support, or by deeply questioning the "weaker" person to encourage them to play a stronger role. The latter is usually done in caucus.

Any attempt by the mediator to balance the power between parties must proceed with care, particularly in interpersonal disputes where the parties' relationship will continue after the mediation. This relationship existed prior to the mediator's intervention and will continue afterwards, without the intervention of the mediator. A mediator should be mindful of this.

On the international level, serious power differences exist between countries and they must continue a productive relationship regardless of the difference. Therefore, a

---

15 Charles A. Kerr, In Mediation What Am I?, The Alternative Dispute Resolution Center of Snohomish and Island Counties, Everett, Washington (Spring 1993).

mediator would be unwise to tamper with the "power relationship," but should aid the parties to reach agreement within the confines of their relationship.

Applications

Mediation is not the magic solution for all conflicts. While some proponents believe mediation should be utilized for all cases, most agree that mediation is effective when at least one of the following criteria is present: where there is an ongoing relationship, business or personal, between the parties; where more than just the disputants need to participate, i.e., children, teachers, etc.; where flexibility in process and/or agreement is needed; where privacy is important; or where the disputants do not wish to set precedents. Situations in which mediation is less likely to be successful are where there are clashing values or principles; where a party wants to be vindicated; where there is a history of violence between the parties; or where a party is not competent due to mental condition, drugs, or alcohol. These sets of criteria describe conflicts that are at opposite ends of the spectrum, and there are many disputes that fall in between and would be amenable to mediation.

As indicated in the beginning of this chapter, mediation has been used to resolve a broad range of disputes. They could be categorized in a number of ways, but here they are arranged by the subject matter of the dispute or the setting within which it occurs. Some of these categories necessarily overlap, and others are in a state of expansion.

Community Disputes

Disputes at the local level can involve seemingly minor issues between community members, such as an individual playing her radio loudly or not controlling the behavior of her children. However, builtup frustration sometimes exaggerates such disputes and results in violence if the problem is not addressed. These are the types of conflicts that find their way into municipal or small claims court or community justice centers. Today many courts are introducing mediation as an alternative to litigation to settle such community disputes.

Sometimes, however, neighborhood disputes are not even the type of problem that can be handled by a court. "Realistically, a large portion of the conflicts brought to dispute centers never would have appeared in court. Either prosecutors would not have bothered to bring charges in many of the less serious cases between family members or neighbors, or there would have been no effective judicial remedy."[16] Across the nation. Community Mediation Centers have sprung up over the last 25 years to handle such

---

16 Singer, *supra* note 7, at 117.

disputes. Mediators in community centers and at the lower court levels are frequently volunteer laypeople.

Another type of community mediation can be used when community groups are in deep conflict, such as when the police department and the residents of a particular neighborhood dispute allegations of unwarranted police force. In those cases, an outside professional mediator frequently is brought in to lessen tensions, explore the problems and their sources, and develop a long-term plan to resolve those problems.

School Mediation

Teaching children and young people to mediate their conflicts is a growing area of education. The Education section of the Association for Conflict Resolution (http://www.mediate.com/acreducation/) is one organization that actively supports integrating mediation into the school systems, from elementary school through college. School mediation involves training students to serve as peer mediators when a conflict arises between other students. Such school mediation programs have proven successful in helping students to develop new skills and "to reduce school violence, to provide an alternative to suspension, and, perhaps most importantly, to help students learn ways of responding to conflict other than by fighting or dropping out."[17]

Some teacher education programs now train teachers in mediation techniques so that they can pass these skills on to their students.[18]

Mediation and Conflict Resolution are actively utilized on college and university campuses. An excellent location for information, including journal articles, on mediation in higher education is http://campus-adr.org.

Criminal Mediation

Although not as popular as community mediation, criminal mediation can take a number of forms, including victim offender confrontations and mediation of domestic violence.

> In still another adaptation of community mediation by the courts both juvenile delinquents and convicted adults are participating in mediation with their victims to work out mutually acceptable sentences to be recommended jointly to the judge. In most of these programs both the defendant and the victim, who may be a representative of a store or other business, must volunteer for mediation. Mediators are community volunteers or, occasionally, probation or parole officers.

---

17   Singer, *supra* note 7, at 155.

18   Such a program exists at Columbia Teachers College, New York City.

Agreements generally include some sort of restitution to the victim, in the form of money or services, or service to the community instead of or in addition to imprisonment. Offenses for which sentences have been mediated range from burglary and drunk driving to armed assault and manslaughter. Both victims and offenders report satisfaction with the process, with victims saying they appreciated the opportunity to describe directly to the offender how the crime changed their lives and to suggest their own remedies.[19]

For more information on victim-offender mediation, see http://voma.org and http://vorp.org.

Mediation of Civil Matters

Within the court system, mediation of civil law suits covers a broad range of topics at both the state and federal levels. The federal courts and some state courts have encouraged mediation through court rules. In some jurisdictions, mediation is being used for cases that are on appeal, so mediation need not be limited to the trial level.

Mediation of Family Matters

Although domestic issues generally are covered under civil law, family mediation is an area requiring separate treatment. Divorce mediation is done by private mediators as well as through the court system. Both attorneys and mental health professionals serve in this area to develop a settlement agreement that can be incorporated into a judgment of divorce. Some court systems mandate mediation of all or at least a portion of a divorce matter, such as child custody and visitation. Mediation of postjudgment disputes is particularly important.

Intra-family disputes are mediated as well, generally through the local community centers. "Conflict within families, whether they occur between parents and teens over adjusting to clashing lifestyles, between adult siblings over caring for elderly parents, or between separating spouses over children or property, spotlight most vividly the advantages and occasional pitfall of negotiated or mediated settlements."[20] Guardianship mediation is also a growing field. Other examples of potential family-oriented conflict include will contests, disagreement over jointly owned property, and the breaking up of a family business. It is clear that such conflicts can be heavily laden with emotional as well as legal issues. And because there is often an ongoing

---

19   Singer, *supra* note 7, at 125, 126.

20   Singer, *supra* note 7, at 31.

relationship to be considered, mediation would appear to be the most appropriate process for seeking a mutually arrived at settlement.

Mediation of Administrative Matters

Administrative matters are those that come before administrative agencies and administrative courts, both state and federal. Mediation is a part of this process as well. The Americans with Disabilities Act and Equal Employment Opportunity Act are two examples of federal legislation that provide for mediation. See the agency website for more comprehensive information.

Similarly,

> [p]arents and school administrators are using mediation to deal with disagreements over educating handicapped children. . . . The purpose: to avoid costly, time-consuming, and emotionally draining administrative hearings that are permitted annually under the Education for All Handicapped Children Act. . . . Although no form of dispute settlement other than court or formal administrative hearings is mentioned in the statute, a growing number of states are devoting significant resources to mediating disputes over special education.[21]

Labor Relations

Many people think that arbitration is the preferred method of conflict resolution in labor disputes. But the area of labor relations is changing, and the old ways of resolving disputes are giving way to mediation. Because of its flexibility and maintenance of relationships between the disputing parties, mediation is an area growing in recognition. Labor relations provides an ADR arena that involves many nonlawyers as neutrals who have specialty training in labor issues. The United States has a federal agency which provides mediation and arbitration services. See, *http://www.fmcs.gov.*

Construction Mediation

Construction is another field previously dominated by arbitration. However, as more contracts contain mediation clauses and more participants convey their satisfaction with nonadjudicative processes, construction mediation will continue to grow. As in labor, the neutral is most likely a specialist in the construction field rather than an attorney. This industry is also utilizing a modified version of mediation called "partnering," in which the two parties collaborate to resolve the problems they have in

---

21 Singer, *supra* note 7, at 157.

common. (See "Building Success for the 21st Century: A Guide to Partnering in the Construction Industry." American Arbitration Association (1996).)

Environmental Mediation

This highly public area of conflict has found mediation particularly appropriate, as attested to by the Environment and Public Policy Section of the Association for Conflict Resolution. Large environmental disputes are frequently multi-partied, multi-issued, and lengthy. One of the goals is to give as many interested constituents as possible the opportunity to participate in the process and the development of a resolution. Such a resolution may be one that the court would have difficulty creating and enforcing. The mediator may be a nonlawyer, but she is frequently someone with specialized expertise in environmental issues.

Commercial Mediation

The use of mediation for commercial disputes continues to expand. As in other areas, the best time to mediate business disputes is in the early stages of the conflict, "before disagreements have escalated, before disputants have incurred the costs of preparing a case for trial, perhaps even before they have hired lawyers."[22]

The types of issues that result in conflict in the business setting include conflicts arising out of commercial activities, such as contracts, within partnerships, complaints by minority shareholders of closely held corporations, takeovers of smaller business by large corporate acquirers, mergers, and policy conflicts. Again, mediation is particularly appropriate because it affords privacy, flexibility, and cost containment. Moreover, and perhaps most importantly, it permits the business relationship to continue.

International Mediation

Historians and political scientists can describe numerous settlements of international disputes, both public and private, aided by mediation. Among the issues dealt with by international mediation are border disputes, trade considerations, and long-standing international conflicts. One of the most prominent historic international mediations was the Camp David meetings and resultant accord.[23] Mediation has been used in Sri Lanka, Nepal, Venezuela, Sudan and Uganda, and Israel/Palestine, among others. Diplomats and other governmental officials are trained in dispute resolution techniques, and former President Jimmy Carter has established the Carter Center,

---

22 Singer, *supra* at 75.

23 Raiffa, *supra* note 5, at 205-217.

which focuses on international conflict resolution, including election monitoring, health care, and peace programs. For more information see http://www.cartercenter.org.

Ethics

In 1994, the Model Standards of Conduct for Mediators were developed by the ABA, the American Arbitration Association (AAA), and the Society for Professionals in Dispute Resolution (SPIDR). In 2005, the ABA, AAA, and the Association for Conflict Resolution made revisions to those standards, which are in Appendix A. They stress the need for self-determination of the parties, impartiality of the neutral, maintaining confidentiality, avoiding conflicts of interest, and providing competent mediators, among others.

Self-Determination

The parties must be able to participate fully in the process and reach a voluntary, uncoerced agreement. In mandatory mediation, which is sometimes a prerequisite to proceeding with a court action, generally the mandate applies to an orientation session explaining the process but does not require participation in the process.

Impartiality

The mediator must remain impartial, evenhanded, and avoid even the appearance of partiality toward either of the parties. Such impartiality requires avoiding mediator prejudice based on race, color, creed, national origin, age, sex, and sexual orientation.[24]

Confidentiality

The parties should discuss their expectations of confidentiality and establish what level of confidentiality they wish maintained. Absent an agreement to the contrary, or a legal exception, most people assume that everything stated during a mediation should remain confidential and not available to the public. In addition, the parties need to be informed regarding the function and confidentiality of the caucus (private sessions). Anything that is said in a caucus cannot be revealed to other parties without the consent of the party with whom the mediator caucuses.

Confidentiality restrictions apply to the parties and the mediator.

Courts faced with the issue generally have concluded that mediators need not testify. They have based their reasoning either on the long tradition (often

---

24   Standards of Conduct for Mediators §11 (see Appendix A).

incorporated into court rules) providing confidentiality for settlement offers or on the threatened danger to neutrality if the mediator should be forced to testify for one of the parties.[25]

See Appendix A, Model Standards of Conduct for Mediators, Standard V, for additional information regarding confidentiality.

Conflicts of Interests

A mediator is required to disclose to the parties any actual or potential conflicts of interest that she may have with the parties. If the parties wish to continue with that mediator after being so informed, the mediation can proceed, unless the nature of the conflict of interest itself casts serious doubt on the integrity of the process. For example, even though a mediator may know one of the parties professionally, the mediation may still proceed if the parties do not object. If, however, the mediation is between a physician and a dissatisfied patient over possible malpractice and the mediator had previously been a patient of the physician, that relationship creates too strong an impression of possible bias. A mediator should also avoid any subsequent relationship with a party.

A mediator must be sensitive to the fact that her employing agency wants to demonstrate high settlement statistics to justify the continued use of mediation. Further, the mediator's own drive to succeed may pressure her to settle as many cases as possible. However, the mediator must take care that the desire on her part or her employer's part to have a high settlement to case mediated ratio does not interfere with her professionalism and commitment to the parties' self-determination.

Competence

The degree and formality of training for mediators and supervision of the mediation process are not settled issues. Education and experience, both in the dispute resolution process and sometimes in the subject matter of the dispute, are very important and must be considered in the selection of a mediator. Unfortunately, the public is not well informed regarding mediator qualifications and may not be in a position to make an informed choice.

The parties' informed choice of a mediator and their satisfaction with the mediator's qualifications is part of the goal of self-determination in alternative dispute resolution. In court-administered or court-referred programs, the court regulates the minimal training and educational requirements of the mediator. Unless there is

---

25   Singer, *supra* note 7, at 174 (*citing* NLRB v. Macaluso, 618 F.2d 51 (9th Cir. 1980)).

state licensing, however, anyone can offer to mediate a conflict privately outside of the court system. It is therefore incumbent upon the mediator to truthfully inform the public as to her qualifications and to refuse to participate in any mediation for which she believes herself to be unprepared or unqualified to mediate.

Another concern is the ongoing supervision and continuing education of mediators. Mediation is a private process, observed only by the neutral and the parties. Since the parties are generally unsophisticated regarding the process, they may be unable to judge the quality of the intervening neutral. Mediators should participate in periodic continuing education, supervised mediation, and related professional development. This will help the mediator overcome the sense of isolation that she experiences and cause her to refine her skills, avoid bad habits, and learn new areas or techniques.

Illegal Agreements

What does a mediator do when he realizes that the parties have reached a solution that is either illegal or against public policy? Examples of an illegal agreement would be divorcing parties' agreeing to call alimony child support for tax benefits, and an agreement between the seller and purchaser of real estate to defraud a lender by setting a higher than actual value on a piece of property. Some would say that it is the parties' agreement and not the concern of the mediator. However, most professionals agree that a mediator faced with such a dilemma can first attempt to explain to the parties that they are reaching what appears to be an illegal contract and urge them to reconsider their agreement. If they refuse, then the neutral should not participate in the settlement process. He can withdraw from the mediation at this point, leaving the door open for further mediation if the parties agree.

Appropriate Parties and Unrepresented Interests

What should a mediator do if she believes that the parties attending the mediation session are not in fact the parties who properly should be present, e.g., when parents appear at the session when their children should be there, when a party is represented by someone who lacks the authority to commit to an agreement, or when one constituency affected by an environmental mediation is not present? Take the case of a community dispute over the behavior of someone's twelve-year-old child. Should the child be present? the parent? both? Can the parent make an agreement that is binding on the child? The mediator can ask that the absent party join the session at a reconvened time. If that is not feasible, the mediator can proceed based on the premise that even nonparties can benefit from the mediation and convey the information to the real parties. Whether or not to proceed should be left to the discretion of the parties or their representatives who are present, since it is their dispute and their process.

Similar to the aforementioned is the issue of unrepresented parties whose interests may be affected by the mediation. Examples are the aged, infants, and other potentially disenfranchised groups. The mediator may suggest that those interests be represented by an additional person invited to the mediation. Some say the mediator is responsible to protect those interests. However, to do so may adversely affect the mediator's neutrality and slow the process. Most would agree that the mediation should proceed, even if unrepresented parties are not present, with an attempt to bring their needs before those who are present and suggest that they be considered in any agreement.

> Which people should be at the table and who should represent whom. . . . Mediators debate vigorously among themselves about the extent of their responsibility to bring such unrepresented constituencies to the bargaining table. There is consensus, however, that if groups believe they have been excluded unfairly, their lack of participation will undercut any agreements reached in their absence.[26]

Power Imbalances

A serious power imbalance between the disputants can create an ethical issue for the mediator. Should a mediation proceed where there is a significant power imbalance between the parties? This will depend on the skill and subjective judgment of the mediator as well as the setting (international disputants rarely share equal power). Can the parties benefit from participation in the process even with the power imbalance? Is the imbalance even an issue? Can the mediator rectify the imbalance? Should the mediator attempt to balance out the power distribution?

A mediator can use the private setting of a caucus to try to overcome the effects of one party's intimidation or lack of assertiveness.

> In extreme cases, however, there are legitimate concerns about whether it is useful — or even appropriate — to attempt to mediate when resources, knowledge, or political power clearly is unequal (in a dispute between a car owner and General Motors, for example). In these circumstances, two questions need to be answered: whether it is possible to educate the less savvy parties about the process . . . and whether some access to expertise (legal or technical advice, for example) can be furnished to those who do not have it otherwise available. . . . The difficulty with declining to mediate in a situation of power imbalances is that mediation may be at least as well suited to the task as are any other available alternatives.[27]

---

26 Singer, *supra* note 7, at 132-133.

27 *Id.* at 177.

Language

How does a mediator deal with non-English speaking disputants? Should there be an official interpreter or should one utilize the family member or friend that the party often brings? Generally, a non-official interpreter will not translate directly and may intersperse her own personal feelings and interpretations. This greatly complicates communication, which is an essential element of the process. The interpreter can be instructed to interpret precisely what is said and not to editorialize; but because the interpreter is not a trained professional, this instruction may have to be repeated throughout the mediation. However, if it is the only way to proceed, and the parties desire, then mediation should proceed. The ideal situation is to utilize the services of a professional interpreter, who may be more readily available in a court setting.

Disclosure of Criminal Activity

What should a mediator do if a crime is disclosed during the mediation session? If it is a past crime, there is no requirement to disclose it. While the mediator may have been told of an act that appears to be a crime, it is not the role of the mediator to sit as judge and jury to determine if there was actually a crime committed. If it is a declaration that the party will commit a future crime, and the mediator is an attorney, she must report it under the attorney's Code of Professional Responsibility. The Model Standards of Conduct for Mediators in Appendix A, Standard VI, A9, and B, also address criminal activity disclosed and indicate that "the mediator shall take appropriate steps including, if necessary, postponing, withdrawing from or terminating the mediation." The mediator's pre-mediation agreement or opening statement should include any such limits on confidentiality.

Summary

Mediation is a dispute resolution process that involves the intervention of a third-party neutral to facilitate the disputing parties' negotiations. It is a flexible process and may take many forms. There are, however, certain invariables. The mediator must be neutral and must be knowledgeable and skilled in the mediation process. The parties should, at a minimum, be amenable to hearing about the process and, optimally, be prepared to negotiate.

The varied forms presented here include facilitative mediation, evaluative mediation, transformative mediation, single-text mediation, and co-mediation. The process, to some degree, is as diverse as those who use it and those who serve as neutrals. The major difference among the various forms of mediation is the degree of the neutral's participation in formulating an agreement — from a neutral who only facilitates communication to one who makes suggestions and urges resolution.

The mediation process can be broken into three general steps. The first is the opening which includes the mediator statement as well as the parties' initial statements and other information gathering. The second step is facilitated negotiation, which includes brainstorming, reality testing, and determining the parties' real interests, and negotiating their interests. Finally, there is a closing, in which the parties reach and affirm an agreement, in whole or in part, or suspend the mediation.

A competent mediator must possess excellent facilitative and interpersonal skills. The former include well-developed, nonjudgmental communication skills enhanced by active listening and the ability to be affirming of a person's emotional communications. Among the interpersonal skills the mediator must have are the ability to guide without forcing, to aid in creative thinking, to provide face-saving techniques and a safe environment, and to keep the process moving and the parties focused.

Neutrality is an important aspect of mediation. The mediator must give the appearance of lack of bias and must avoid a conflict of interest. While maintaining neutrality, a mediator may also have to consider power imbalances between the parties, whether it is appropriate to intervene in the power picture, and whether that intervention adversely affects neutrality.

Mediation is being applied in a growing number of diverse subject areas. Mediation originated in the community-based programs and continues to provide services in that area. Peer mediation is being used in public and parochial schools as well as colleges and universities. The court systems use mediation in criminal victim-offender programs, in civil matters including a significant emphasis on family mediation, and in administrative law matters. In the commercial area, mediation is used for labor-management disputes, construction disputes, environmental disputes, and general business conflicts. Many of these areas where mediation has been put to good use have grown out of contracts authorizing use of the mediation process. Particularly unique models of mediation are utilized in international mediation.

Ethical considerations must be closely monitored. The ABA, AAA, and ACR have developed joint standards of conduct for mediators which include issues of party self-determination, impartiality of the mediator, confidentiality of the process (with limitations), avoidance of conflicts of interest, and mediator competence.

In addition, mediators must avoid illegal settlement agreements, ensure the appropriate parties are at the mediation table, and deal with power imbalances between the parties.

Sensitivity to cultural as well as linguistic diversity can be important in some mediations.

EXERCISES

1. Research the court-annexed mediation available in your state or county. List the types of courts where it is used. Is it mandated in any of those courts? Who serves as mediator? Do they use individual mediators or co-mediation?

2. List the private providers of mediation services in your area. Who serves as mediator? What is the cost? What types of conflicts do they mediate? Do they use individual mediators or a panel?

3. Observe a mediation and report on the skills the mediator used, including presentation of the opening statement. Describe the conflict and the results of the mediation.

4. Research your state's Rules of Professional Conduct and Ethics Opinions for attorneys and determine the following:

    a. Can attorneys serve as mediators and then prepare the mediated agreement?

    b. Can attorneys offer mediation services out of their law offices?

    c. Have any other ethical issues regarding mediation come before the Ethics Committee in your state and, if so, what was the issue and the outcome?

5. In your state, are there any educational or training requirements for individuals doing court-annexed (or court-referred) mediation? If so, what are they?

6. If you know anyone who has participated in a mediation, interview them about how they view and evaluate the process and the results.

7. Prepare a written opening statement and then present it to the class.

8. Research the use of either Guardianship Mediation or Child Welfare (or Child Protection) Mediation and discuss your findings in class.

9. Study the utilization of mediation in either international or environmental conflict and determine the model followed, the historical context, the power distribution, and the outcome.

Mediation Role Plays

Neighborhood Dispute (four individuals, two parties)

John and Jossie Tarnet are a married couple who are in their mid-40s, and one year ago they moved into a downtown location of a desirable urban community. The homes are newer, but the lots relatively small (50-to 75-feet wide), making some contact with neighbors unavoidable. Both John and Jossie are professionals, but enjoy caring for their home and the yard. They have two adult children living with them, a 21-year-old son named Sigi and a 23-year-old daughter named Mary. Both children work and attend college. On one side of the Tarnets live Jake and Eustice Johnson, an older couple who have been in the neighborhood a long time and who are friendly with the Tarnets. There is an old fence between the properties, but it is not of much use.

The properties are not sunny due to the presence of numerous trees. The older couple has started a vegetable garden in the front yard, because there is absolutely no sun in the small rear yard. This has greatly distressed the Tarnets. They believe it is an inappropriate use of the front yard and has an adverse effect on the appearance of the neighborhood, which generally consists of small, well-manicured lawns. One day, the Tarnet's dog was unattended in the yard and wandered over to the neighbors' garden and used it as her bathroom. The neighbors did not see this, but saw the results and believed it to be the work of the Tarnet's dog. Several weeks later, coming home late one night and very tired from a full day at work and school, Mary turned too widely into the driveway and ended up partially in the Johnson's vegetable garden, further damaging it. The next day she went over to apologize to the Johnsons, but they refused to listen to her or anyone from the Tarnet household because they had come to believe that the Tarnet family is actively sabotaging their garden.

One Saturday morning at about 8:30, the Tarnets were out doing their yard work and using a gas-powered leaf blower to blow the driveway clean of grass clippings. Suddenly, the police showed up and issued a summons for disturbing the peace and violating the local noise ordinance. The Tarnets surmised that the Johnsons had called the police and reported them. They had thought the misunderstanding would eventually resolve itself; instead it seemed to be escalating. Mrs. Tarnet had heard about a community mediation center and decided to give this new thing a try. She called the center and asked them to intervene.

The center wrote a letter to both parties, scheduling a meeting on a weeknight to inform them about the process and how the community center works. Both couples arrive and view the introductory videotape and agree to meet with you, the mediator.

Women in College (two mediators, six parties)

The college newspaper contained a large drawing of several very sexy semi-nude women wrestling with each other. Under it was the caption, "All the women are fighting for DXE men." It was intended to catch the eye of males who might be interested in pledging for DXE, a men's social fraternity that was seeking new members. In the same issue was an article by one of the male students on the editorial staff, Rock Tames, raging against the concept of "date rape," arguing that in his opinion, there was no such thing. This was in response to an announcement of a date rape seminar in the previous week's publication.

A number of women on campus were outraged by both the drawing and the article and brought the material to several feminist faculty members on campus. The Women's Center had an emergency meeting to discuss the problem. Before the meeting, the president of DXE was contacted to see if he would issue a public apology for the drawing, which the women believed denigrated women and reduced them to sex symbols. He refused to issue an apology, saying it was all done in good fun and that the women were making a big deal out of nothing. The newspaper was also approached and a retraction of the article requested, to no avail. Dr. Janice Wooster brought to the meeting a draft of a letter she wanted to have published in the school paper in response to both the ad and the article, which she claimed indicated strongly felt anti-female sympathies on campus. Her letter was extremely anti-male and strongly worded and the other members said that if it was to officially come from the Women's Center, it had to be toned down and made to sound more rational. They worked on it together and came up with a final draft. When submitted, the school paper refused to print it.

Outraged, representatives of the Women's Center approached the Dean of Students, who called a public meeting of the editorial staff of the newspaper, the students, and faculty from the Women's Center and any other interested parties, including staff. Much to the Dean's surprise, nearly 250 people showed up at the meeting, which quickly turned into such a free-for-all that security had to be called to disband the meeting. The Dean forbade the newspaper to print anything on the subject until the matter was resolved. He did not have the authority to do so, but the paper complied. However, posters started to show up around campus and in the residence halls, calling the Women's Center members "dykey bitches" and the newspaper's staff "chauvinist rapists."

A sociology professor who teaches conflict resolution approached the Dean and suggested that this matter be brought before the newly formed mediation center on campus. She reminded the Dean that the center was comprised of students who had been trained in mediation and who could sit as neutrals to help the parties try to resolve their differences. The Dean was skeptical, but took the idea to the Provost, who by this time was decidedly unhappy about the lack of progress in resolving this issue. The matter had leaked to the outside press and it was creating negative publicity for the college. The Provost indicated that she thought mediation a good idea, so long as co-mediators were used, and so long as the administration was represented at the mediation.

A letter was sent from the Office of the President inviting two representatives from the Women's Center and two representatives from the editorial staff to attend the mediation session. The young man who wrote the article about date rape was also invited. Two mediators were chosen: one white female and one black male. They were chosen for their abilities as well as to ensure a diverse gender and ethnic mix. A Hispanic female from the President's office also was to attend to represent the administration. The press found out about the mediation and wanted to attend, but access was denied.

You are one of the mediators. It is important to meet with the other mediators to determine who will make the opening statement and how the mediation should progress. You are concerned about the volatility of this issue.

Corporate Legal Department (two parties)

Lanex Corporation has an in-house corporate legal department consisting of two secretaries, four paralegals, and three attorneys. There has been a great deal of unrest in the department since the addition of the most recently hired attorney, Shirley Downs. Finally, one of the secretaries, Tammy Whine, filed a personnel grievance with the union indicating that Ms. Downs was treating her unfairly, giving her an unrealistic amount of work, and expecting her to work during breaks and after working hours. Ms. Downs responded that the allegations were untrue and that Ms. Whine was underproducing. Ms. Downs had been hired to replace the former general counsel and to make the department more productive; that was what she was trying to do.

One of the paralegals, Alice Tokla, has put in for a transfer to the contracts department. There is an opening there, but her skills are probably put to better use in the legal department. The company wants to know why she is seeking the transfer — more particularly, whether it is due to the personnel problems in legal.

One of the problems is that the former general counsel was a very likeable guy. However, he had an alcohol problem that was diminishing his ability to work productively. He had attended the Alcoholics Anonymous unit in the company and improved for a while, but he later regressed and refused help. However, none of the people in legal know of his problem, only that he was let go and replaced by Ms. Downs. The entire department was very unhappy with his departure.

Company policy is going to require total computerization of the legal department within three months. Some people, particularly Ms. Whine, are resisting. Almost everyone else is looking forward to it.

In addition to the foregoing, the company is probably going to be bought out by Intex and that may create more problems. Rumors are running wild. Will legal be replaced by Intex's legal department? Will certain corporate sections have to move to Intex's location over 150 miles away? Are their jobs secure? Is Shirley Downs really a spy for Intex? All of the employees' free time is spent discussing these and other scenarios. Everyone is on edge.

The union has brought the grievance to corporate personnel. Both have agreed to have a mediator from the ombuds office meet informally with all individuals in the legal department to gather information and then sit down with Ms. Downs and Ms. Whine to help them work out their differences if possible.

Arbitration

Introduction

> Arbitration, or private decisionmaking, has been used in the United States since its early commercial history. . . . Although its popularity has declined somewhat in favor of newer forms of dispute resolution, which permit the parties to retain some control over the outcome, arbitration still is used predominantly in businesses desiring private, binding decisions by third-party neutrals.[1]

Arbitration is adjudicatory in nature and is the ADR process most like litigation. It is the most used dispute resolution process. A third-party neutral, or panel of neutrals (3 arbitrators), hears each disputant's presentation of his or her case, including sworn testimony and documentary and physical evidence. Frequently, parties are represented by counsel. At the end of the presentations, the neutral makes an award, i.e., decides the case in favor of one party or the other. While the process can be less formal than the courtroom and the arbitrators are not always bound by the rules of evidence or precedent, arbitration is more formal than negotiation or mediation and has its own procedural and substantive rules. It has a long and distinguished history in some areas, such as commercial arbitration and labor disputes. "George Washington, for example, included a provision in his will calling for arbitration of any conflict that might arise over the interpretation of his will and the distribution of his estate."[2]

Arbitration can occur privately or through the court system; the mandate to arbitrate can come from a statute, a court rule, a contract between the disputants, preference of the parties, or custom; and the arbitration can be binding or nonbinding, mandatory or voluntary. These categorizations are not mutually exclusive. For example, one can have private, binding, contractually based arbitration, or one can have court-annexed, nonbinding, statutory based arbitration.

---

1 Linda R. Singer, Settling Disputes: Conflict Resolution in Business, Families, and The Legal System 27 (2d ed. 1994).

2 Susan M. Leeson & Bryan M. Johnston, Ending It: Dispute Resolution in America 48 (1988).

Arbitration will continue to grow as a dispute resolution process because (1) it is private and aids in avoiding publicity; (2) it offers more rapid resolution of conflicts that otherwise would be delayed by crowded court dockets; and (3) it offers the parties some degree of autonomy through the selection of an arbitrator, who is more likely to have subject matter expertise than a judge.

Private and Court-Annexed Arbitration

Private arbitration is a process chosen by the parties outside of the court system. They choose an arbitrator(s) or go through one of the private providers of arbitration services, such as the American Arbitration Association. The parties' dispute and its resolution through the award of the arbitrator is never made part of any public record unless they so desire or it is the custom of their field. The parties themselves pay for the services of the arbitrator.

Court-annexed arbitration takes place in the courthouse by arbitrators provided by the court system and under court authority. The parties have less control over the process, as they do not choose the arbitrators or the arbitration rules to be followed. However, since the parties have little choice in this process, the award is nonbinding. This process does not cost the parties anything unless they appeal it.

How Do Disputants Come to Arbitration?

The most common source of arbitration cases is a contractual agreement. Parties enter into a business contract that provides that if there is a dispute over the contract or the relationship it creates, that dispute will be arbitrated. Some such clauses are general and state simply that "[A]ny difference or dispute arising under this contract will be resolved through arbitration. . . ." Other clauses specifically delineate what matters can be arbitrated.[3] They can further specify controls, such as what rules govern, who serves as arbitrator, and the number of arbitrators. Contract-based arbitration is private.

If the parties do not have a contractual relationship requiring them to arbitrate, they can still agree to use the process. Such arrangements are considered voluntary and usually provide for binding arbitration, which means that the parties are bound by the award of the arbitrator and can only appeal in specified legal contexts.[4]

---

3   *Id.* at 50.

4   For a list of grounds for setting aside an arbitration award by the court, see *infra* at pages 108-109.

Throughout the country, statutory authority and court rules are emerging that require arbitration, particularly in certain classes of cases that are within the court system. An example is the requirement that all cases in trial court involving automobile property damage in excess of $10,000 must go to arbitration. This type of arbitration is court-annexed and nonbinding.

The labor field is governed by both custom and contract and it relies extensively on private, binding arbitration for resolution of disputes. Examples of labor issues frequently arbitrated include private employee matters, public employee salaries, and sports figures' salaries.

Binding and Nonbinding Arbitration

"Binding arbitration" means that the arbitrator's award is final and generally not appealable. It is found in the private sector and is entered into by agreement or custom. The arbitrator's authority in binding arbitration comes from the terms of the contract or agreement that brings the parties to the arbitration forum and his award is governed by that same contract. The courts traditionally have honored binding arbitration awards and rarely overturned them, doing so on very limited grounds.

Nonbinding arbitration, on the other hand, is mandated by the court or is court-annexed. In this type of dispute resolution, the parties are notified, after initial pleadings are filed with the court, to appear before an arbitrator to present their case. At the end of this hearing, the arbitrator makes an award. If the parties are satisfied with the arbitrator's award, it becomes a judgment after a specified period of time. If either party is dissatisfied and so notifies the court within that specified time, there is a trial de novo[5] of the matter. There is usually a penalty for requesting a trial de novo, such as payment of a fee, or a penalty if one is not more successful in court than they were in arbitration. One must also consider the additional time and cost involved in continuing through the judicial process.

It concerns some consumer advocates that nonbinding arbitration might be seen as just an additional step litigants have to take before getting to court, and in this respect has a chilling effect on a party's interest in litigating. However, others point out that the dispute is processed more quickly in arbitration and that benefits the parties. One of the drawbacks of nonbinding arbitration is that some seasoned litigants or their representatives take it less seriously than a court hearing and therefore prepare less for the arbitration and appear to be just "going through the motions."

---

5 Literally, "from the beginning," as if the arbitration had not taken place.

Mandatory or Voluntary Arbitration

Whether arbitration is mandatory or voluntary determines whether the parties are required to participate in arbitration or choose to do so. Generally court-ordered or court-annexed arbitration, based in statute or court rules, is mandatory arbitration, i.e., the parties do not have a choice. Contractual arbitration or that arising out of custom is considered voluntary, since it arises out of the initial voluntary act of entering into a contract. Likewise, if parties find themselves in a dispute and choose private arbitration, their process is considered voluntary.

To summarize the foregoing, a dispute over a contract that contains an arbitration clause will proceed to private, binding arbitration, which is voluntary and governed by the contract. A matter in which a complaint has been filed in court, which falls under the statute requiring arbitration, will be arbitrated in the courthouse and the arbitration is considered mandatory and nonbinding. It can generally be said that if arbitration is mandatory or court-annexed, it is nonbinding; and if it is voluntary and private, it is binding. Note, however, some of the exceptions that follow.

Applications

Labor Relations

Labor arbitration is considered voluntary and binding.

Most states . . . have enacted statutes requiring arbitration of labor-management disputes, particularly those involving public sector employees such as teachers, police, and firefighters. Today over 90 percent of all collective bargaining agreements specify arbitration for the resolution of disputes. . . .

Arbitration in the labor-management context can take two forms. One is called interest arbitration, which occurs when the parties have reached impasse in the collective bargaining process. If they cannot agree to the terms of a contract through negotiation or mediation, an arbitrator can be called in to declare what the rights of the respective parties will be under the proposed contract. The second form is called grievance arbitration. It occurs when a dispute arises under an existing contract and the parties cannot agree about the meaning or significance of the terms.[6]

---

6 Leeson & Johnston, *supra* note 2, at 49.

When the labor dispute is one involving public service employees such as fire fighters or the police, the form of arbitration is compulsory, binding, and interest-based, as opposed to voluntary, nonbinding, and grievance-based. In disputes involving professional sports figures, both salary and grievance arbitration are used, and "final offer" arbitration (see page 106) is particularly favored.

Commercial Arbitration

Commercial arbitration occurs on an international level, on a national level, and on the local level. "The International Chamber of Commerce, the American Arbitration Association, and the State of Hawaii are among those competing for the international commercial dispute resolution business."[7] It is usually contract-based and business-oriented.

> Arbitration has broad applicability in business. Where parties want to submit their dispute to an expert in their own business, they generally will use arbitration; where there is a continuing relationship between parties which they can't afford to rupture, they will provide for arbitration to decide their disputes; where there is a practical need for a prompt and final decision, businesspeople often arbitrate.[8]

Commercial arbitration is binding.

Court-Annexed Arbitration

This is a growing area of practice. It is usually the creature of statute or court rule, both of which can

> establish criteria that identify cases eligible for arbitration. Disputants whose cases fit these criteria must participate in arbitration as a prerequisite to trial. In contrast, commercial arbitration has traditionally been available as an option for litigants who wished to escape the civil trial track. A secondary distinction between commercial arbitration and CAA [court-annexed arbitration] is that CAA is mandatory but nonbinding; all arbitration decisions may be appealed. On the other hand, commercial arbitration, entered into voluntarily, is binding upon the parties to a dispute.[9]

---

7   *Id.* at 49.

8   Robert Coulson, How to Stay Out of Court 145 (1985).

9   John P. McIver & Susan Keilitz, Court-Annexed Arbitration: An Introduction, 13 Just. Sys No 2, 123 (1991).

Court-annexed arbitration programs vary within each jurisdiction, as well as from state to state. "The principal procedural dimension that distinguishes CAA programs [from one another] appears to be whether the program's procedural rules are geared to increase the speed of civil dispute resolution. Some programs place strict time limits on all aspects of pre- and post-hearing procedures while others are much more permissive."[10] For example, parties to a CAA may have a 30-day time period within which to appeal the award and request a trial de novo.

> [E]ach of the state court-annexed arbitration programs contains some provision for reconsideration of the arbitration decision. Any party may appeal the decision by requesting a trial de novo. The state restrictions on re-entry into the civil litigation track vary primarily in terms of time limits for filing an appeal and disincentives to appealing the arbitration decision. These disincentives most commonly come in the form of fees to appeal and potential liability for costs of the arbitration if the appellant does not appeal and potential liability for costs of the arbitration if the appellant does not improve his or her position at trial. They are designed to ensure . . . participation in the arbitration process and to encourage the conclusion of the litigation. Without disincentives to appeal, CAA could be viewed by attorneys and litigants as simply another discovery device rather than as a viable technique for ending the dispute.[11]

Arbitration is also a part of the federal judicial system.

> Arbitration is expected in civil actions [federal] in which the relief sought involves only monetary damages of $100,000 or less, exclusive of interest and legal expenses. The district courts are to presume that civil actions fall within the boundaries of this program unless counsel certifies otherwise. Procedural rules established by legislation include the requirements that:
>
> - hearings take place within 180 days of the answer to the complaint;
> - trial de novo is guaranteed;
> - a request for trial de novo must be filed within 30 days of the filing of the arbitration award;
> - a trial de novo case must be restored to the court docket as if it had not been arbitrated;

---

10   *Id.* at 127.

11   McIver & Keilitz, *supra* note 9, at 127.

- arbitration evidence and results are sealed to district court judge until the conclusion of the trial de novo.[12]

Consumer Disputes

Consumer arbitration covers a wide variety of disputes between consumers and providers, such as the automobile industry, the insurance industry, or the securities industry. The Better Business Bureau and the Federal Trade Commission are both providers of consumer arbitration. One area of consumer arbitration — disputes over new cars that are found unsatisfactory by the consumer — has been expanded through the enactment of "lemon laws." These

> entitle consumers to a rebate or a new car if they have recurring complaints during the warranty period [and they] require consumers to go to an arbitration program if it meets certain prescribed standards, before suing the manufacturer. Some states, including Conn., Mass., and Maryland, have responded by setting up their own mediation and arbitration programs. In Connecticut, arbitration panels use an independent expert to advise them on technical issues in order to balance the manufacturers' technical advantage.[13]

Other consumer disputes may reach arbitration through contract.

> Stockbrokers, automobile manufacturers, moving companies, law firms and health care organizations are examples of groups that commonly include arbitration clauses in their agreements with clients. Likewise, many insurance companies and their policyholders rely on arbitration to resolve uninsured motorist, extent of coverage, and other claims.[14]

Builders of new homes frequently provide purchasers with certain warranties and include arbitration as a process to remedy the breach therof.

Other Applications

Many state environmental agencies and the federal Environmental Protection Agency (EPA) utilize the arbitration process. The Association for Conflict Resolution has an Environment and Public Policy Section. Both environmental and public policy

---

12 *Id.* at 131-132.

13 Singer, *supra* note 1, at 89-90.

14 Leeson & Johnston, *supra* note 2, at 49.

practices range from small group to large multiparty cases, from site-specific to regulatory negotiations. On the international level, there is an International Court of Environmental Arbitration and Conciliation (ICEAC). Intellectual property (patents, trademark, and licensing) disputes are also submitted to arbitration, both within the United States and internationally.

International arbitration is a "term that embodies both arbitration of disputes between states and international commercial arbitration, usually between private entities residing in different countries."[15] Regarding arbitration between states, "nation-states or other entities recognized by international law may agree to resolve their disputes through international arbitration as established by preexisting obligations under international law, such as a treaty, or by agreement after the dispute arises."[16]

Understanding the Process

Preparation

Preparing for arbitration is like preparing for litigation. Discovery should be complete, evidence must be in order, witnesses should be prepared for testimony, and the attorney must have a thorough knowledge of the facts, the underlying contract, if any, and any applicable law. It is extremely frustrating for the arbitrator, or one's adversary, to be faced with an unprepared attorney. It shows a lack of respect for the process and may be construed as an attempt to use the arbitration proceeding as a discovery tool or an opportunity to delay.

In some private arbitrations, there is occasionally an exchange of preliminary "pleadings," such as a Demand for Arbitration and an Answer and possible counterclaim. The documents are in written form and submitted to the sponsoring agency as well as to the opposing parties; they are brief in nature. The demand, for example, includes an outline of the dispute and the amount of damages or other remedy sought.

Either the parties will have chosen the arbitrator from a list supplied to them or, if they are unable to agree, the sponsoring agency will have chosen an arbitrator for them. There may have been a preliminary hearing to establish discovery deadlines and schedule hearings and other preparatory matters. The parties may also have exchanged information, like witness lists.

---

15   Douglas H. Yarn, ed., *Dictionary of Conflict Resolution* at 230 (1999).

16   *Id.* at 31, 32.

Procedure

While each arbitration is unique, a basic format is followed. The hearing does not take place in a courtroom, but in a "hearing" room. The arbitrator (or arbitrators) introduces herself and determines the names of all present and the role they play. Anyone who is going to testify is sworn in by the arbitrator. If necessary, the arbitration process is explained so that the participants know what to expect. In some instances, the hearing is recorded by a court reporter, although usually the arbitrator maintains a record of the hearing. The record includes the names and addresses of witnesses and copies of all documentary evidence submitted. All evidence is marked as in a trial.

The attorneys, or the parties themselves, can make opening statements, which include a summary of their side of the dispute. This is followed by the testimony of witnesses and the introduction of documentary and other physical evidence. The party demanding the arbitration presents his case first, followed by the opposing party. Each side has the opportunity to cross-examine and provide rebuttal testimony as in a trial. While the hearing is not bound by the rules of evidence, such rules can be used as a guidepost. Upon completion of the presentation of each side's case, the attorneys or parties are given the opportunity to make closing arguments. The arbitrator may request that the attorneys brief — i.e., prepare a detailed, written argument — a particular legal issue. Once all factual and legal issues are presented, the hearing is closed, after which the arbitrator has a stipulated period of time in which to render an award. Sometimes a party will request that a hearing be reopened to consider new evidence.

Arbitrations can be very brief — as short as one hour — or can take an extended period of time. The arbitrator can be an attorney, or an expert in the field that is the subject matter of the dispute. In some instances, the disputing parties retain control over the process and over the standards used in resolving the dispute.[17] "Parties who have not agreed beforehand to submit their dispute to arbitration can elect the process after a dispute arises."[18] In private arbitration, the arbitrator's fee is paid by the parties.

Final-Offer Arbitration

Some states require final-offer or last-offer arbitration. It is a popular vehicle in professional sports salary negotiations.

> With minor modifications, it works as follows. Negotiations are divided into two phases. In Phase 1 the parties bargain directly with or without the aid of an

---

17   Leeson & Johnston, *supra* note 2, at 47.

18   *Id.* at 50.

intervenor (mediator). If the parties agree, there is no second phase. If the parties disagree, the negotiations enter Phase 2, at which point the arbitrator enters the scene. In most states the arbitrator does not obtain guidance or information from the mediator present in Phase 1. The arbitrator determines the facts and then demands from each party a sealed final offer. These final offers are submitted essentially simultaneously, and the arbitrator must then, by law, select one of these two final offers; no in-between compromises are permissible, and the selected final offer becomes binding on both sides. . . . [F]inal offer arbitration is quite effective in persuading parties to settle without an imposed arbitrated solution.[19]

The theory supporting the use of final-offer arbitration is that the parties will be reasonable in their final offer, believing that the arbitrator will choose the most reasonable offer under the circumstances.

Attorney and Paralegal Roles

"Lawyers play three important roles in voluntary arbitration. First, they negotiate and draft contracts. Second, they represent parties in arbitration. Third, they serve as arbitrators."[20] The same is true of paralegals. First, they draft contracts, review contracts, and develop form banks that contain dispute resolution clauses for inclusion in contracts, orders, and agreements. Second, they assist in preparing the matter for arbitration. Third, the paralegal can attend the hearing with the attorney and take notes, provide documents, and in general assist the attorney. Finally, arbitrators need not be attorneys. If a paralegal has a field of specialization, such as real estate, and a professional history in that field, she can combine arbitration training with that specialization and serve as an arbitrator.

The Arbitrator's Role

"The arbitrator or arbitration panel is responsible for the conduct of the hearing. In addition to the general tasks of convening the session and directing the flow of the procedure, the arbitrator has the task of maintaining control over the disputants and their representatives."[21] "A good arbitrator should be decisive, comfortable running a hearing, capable of distinguishing facts from opinions, and, where required, able to write reasoned decisions."[22]

---

19 Howard Raiffa, The Art & Science of Negotiation 110-111 (1982). Reprinted 2005.

20 Leeson & Johnston, *supra* note 2, at 53.

21 *Id.* at 50.

22 Singer, *supra* note 1, at 173.

Someone who is an experienced mediator and who enjoys the mediation process may have difficulty serving as an arbitrator, and vice versa, because the roles are so different. The mediator is a facilitator who brings the parties to their own agreement. The arbitrator hears evidence and decides who will win and who will lose the case, based upon the contract and the law.

The mandatory qualifications of arbitrators vary within jurisdictions and within state programs. For example, in some programs — Arizona, Colorado, and Missouri, among others — lay arbitrators are permitted. Other programs require attorney arbitrators. Still others require attorney arbitrators to have a minimum number of professional years of experience. On the other hand, the field of labor/management arbitration generally does not use attorney arbitrators at all.

Another arbitrator qualification is knowledge of the subject matter and minimum number of years of experience in that field, such as construction, real estate, or labor relations. There are opportunities to serve as a voluntary arbitrator (Better Business Bureau) as well as opportunities for compensated service (American Arbitration Association).

Ethics

The arbitrator is responsible for maintaining the integrity and fairness of the arbitration hearing. This means that the arbitrator must actively demonstrate fairness toward the parties and avoid any hint of bias. It further requires that an arbitrator disclose any potential conflict of interest and avoid any future conflict of interest. For example, an arbitrator should have no financial or personal dealings with either of the parties.

An arbitrator must decide the case within the confines of the contract or the agreement that brought the matter to arbitration, and not exceed that authority. Further, the process should be conducted diligently and without undue delay. The arbitrator must also maintain the confidentiality of the process.

Arbitration awards are generally upheld and enforced when appealed to the court. But courts do have limited power to vacate an arbitration award, granted under the United States Arbitration Act, 9 U.S.C. §§1-14 (1925). Section 10 of the Act states:

> In either of the following cases in the United States[, the] court in and for the district wherein the award was made may make an order vacating the award upon the application of any party to the arbitration —
>
> (a) Where the award was procured by corruption, fraud, or undue means.

(b) Where there was evident partiality or corruption in the arbitrators, or either of them.

(c) Where the arbitrators were guilty of misconduct in refusing to postpone the hearing, upon sufficient cause shown, or in refusing to hear evidence pertinent and material to the controversy; or of any other misbehavior by which the rights of any party have been pre-judged.

(d) Where the arbitrators exceeded their powers, or so imperfectly executed them that a mutual, final and definite award upon the subject matter submitted was not made.

(e) Where an award is vacated and the time within which the agreement required the award to be made has not expired the court may, in its discretion, direct a rehearing by the arbitrators.[23]

Sometimes the court's intervention is sought by a party at the commencement of the arbitration, over the issue of whether a particular contract or a particular issue is subject to arbitration (arbitrability issues). While an arbitrator may decide in favor of or against arbitrability, that decision is considered a matter of law and is reviewable by the courts. Alternatively, if one of the parties originally brings the matter before the court, without proceeding in arbitration, the courts can order the arbitration of a matter that is the subject of an agreement to arbitrate. Courts generally resolve arbitrability issues in favor of arbitration.[24]

Summary

Arbitration is a dispute resolution process that uses a third party to determine the outcome of a dispute; an arbitrator hears the case and makes an award. Arbitration is used extensively in the private sector and is expanding in court-annexed programs. Usually in the former, the process arises out of a contractual obligation and the award is binding, while in the latter, the court mandates arbitration in pending litigation and the award is not binding.

The fields most likely to seek private arbitration of disputes include labor, commerce, and consumer applications in the insurance, securities, and automobile industries, among others. Court-related arbitration can also be found at many levels within

---

23 *Quoted in* Leeson & Johnston, *supra* note 2, at 72-73.

24 See, e.g., Moses M. Cone Memorial Hosp. v. Mercury Const. Corp., 460 U.S. 1, 24-25 (1983).

the federal and state systems. Court-annexed or lawsuit-related arbitration is usually mandated by statute or court rule.

The arbitration hearing itself is similar to a court hearing, but is less formal. The parties and/or their counsel should prepare as they would for a trial. The arbitrator hears opening statements and oral testimony, reviews documentary evidence, and permits oral argument before making an award.

A good arbitrator conducts an efficient and bias-free hearing, pursuant to either contract or statute, and makes a fair and independent award based upon the contract or the law. As part of her ethical responsibility, an arbitrator must avoid any conflict of interest and maintain confidentiality. The court will rarely overturn an arbitration award and limits its review to issues of corruption, fraud, undue influence, evident partiality, misconduct, and instances where the arbitrator exceeded her powers.

EXERCISES

1. Check the statutes of your state to determine if your state has adopted the Uniform Arbitration Act.

2. Are there any reporters that deal specifically with arbitration awards? If so, what are they?

3. Observe an arbitration proceeding and report on it to the class.

4. Where is court-annexed arbitration being used in your state?

5. Are there any private arbitration providers in your area? What credentials do they require of the arbitrators whose services they use?

6. Review the facts and the law in a fact pattern from your litigation class. Choose which side you want to represent and then do the legal research necessary to present the case. Choose a classmate to be your client and prepare them for the arbitration. You and the other attorney should jointly choose an arbitrator from among your classmates. Do a hearing and ask the arbitrator to provide a written award.

7. Do the same as in Exercise 6, but choose a panel of three arbitrators.

Arbitration Role Play

Unpaid Contract

JustAgreement is a for-profit dispute resolution organization that provides private mediation and arbitration services to small businesses in the Midwest. JustAgreement engages mediators and arbitrators as independent contractors on an as-needed basis. The company has a web page, is in the yellow pages, has a page on MySpace, and does presentations regarding ADR at conferences and professional development seminars. The company has been in business for over ten years. It offers experienced and well-educated professionals who serve as neutrals for a variety of cases.

Wonderdust is a small manufacturer of cleaning implements that has been in business for over 20 years. There is an employee who has been unhappy for some time and has indicated to Johnny Moore from Human Resources that he feels the company has been discriminating against him. Johnny has tried to address his issue, but unsuccessfully. In order to avoid litigation, Johnny suggested to the company that they try arbitration with this individual. Reluctantly, the CEO agreed and much to Johnny's surprise, so did the employee. Johnny contacted JustAgreement.

It took quite a bit of time to set up the arbitration. There were misunderstandings about which process Wonderdust was seeking, and scheduling was a problem. However, it was ultimately done.

The arbitration occurred and the arbitrator, Molly Malone, made an award for the employee, although it was not a large financial award. Molly believed that the company representative seemed very upset with the employee's award.

Wonderdust has refused to respond to follow-up inquiries made by JustAgreement and has refused to pay for services rendered in the amount of $2,500. The contract between the parties provides that all disputes arising out of the contract will be resolved through binding arbitration. JustAgreement files a request for arbitration with the local office of a national provider.

Other Forms of Dispute Resolution

Introduction

There are myriad forms of dispute resolution practiced in the United States today. Many follow the guidelines of one of the principal processes we have already considered;[1] others are a combination of the principal models to form a hybrid. For example, when disputants use med-arb, they initially try to resolve their dispute with the assistance of a mediator. If mediation does not result in an agreement, however, the parties proceed to arbitration.

These diverse forms of dispute resolution can be classified as either adjudicative or nonadjudicative. In an adjudicative process, the neutral makes a decision or renders an award finally determining the issues presented. Alternatively, in a nonadjudicative process, the neutral serves as a facilitator/advisor rather than as a decisionmaker. Arbitration is an adjudicative form of dispute resolution and mediation is a nonadjudicative form.

In this chapter, forms of dispute resolution other than the three principal approaches will be defined, examples of them given, and their role in the overall scheme of dispute resolution discussed.

Adjudicative Processes

Adjudicative processes are those in which a decision by a neutral third party is imposed upon the disputants and is enforceable by the state. (For more detail, see "adjudicative processes" in *Dictionary of Conflict Resolution*.) The process can be voluntary or involuntary and the decision binding or nonbinding, depending on the particular process and, sometimes, the desire of the parties.

Private Judging

This is a private process in which the parties agree to employ a third-party neutral to hear and decide their case or ask the court to permit diversion of the case to a private judge. The process is voluntary and binding, and it can be agreed upon when the parties enter into the contract that gives rise to their dispute or at any time thereafter. Private judging is usually chosen when the parties face the imminent prospect of a lengthy trial. In one instance, the parties and their counsel found themselves waiting too long to get a trial date, were concerned they would not get consecutive trial dates, and agreed to hire a retired judge to hear and decide their litigation. The process gives the parties control over the choice of a neutral as well as the scheduling of the hearing and the rules

---

1 Negotiation, mediation, or arbitration.

governing the process. This contributes to a more expedited proceeding with a neutral who has experience in the subject matter.

In some circumstances or jurisdictions, the choice to use a private judge is made entirely by the parties, without court intervention. In other jurisdictions, the court will refer certain cases to a private judge, or the parties can request a court referral to private judging.

> Unlike voluntary arbitration, private judging involves a selection of a "referee" who is empowered by statute to enter a judgment having the finality, precedent value and appealability of a regular trial court decree.[2]
>
> Under "rent-a-judge" statutes, parties file a joint petition with the court in which the case has been filed (known as the presiding court) requesting that the case be tried before a "rented" judge of the parties' selection. Typically, "rented" judges are retired judges or magistrates who know the law and the procedural requirements of a formal trial in that jurisdiction. If the court agrees, the case is assigned to the "rented" judge. The judge follows the jurisdiction's rules of evidence and procedure, and applies the jurisdiction's law in hearing the case. The judge submits findings of fact and conclusions of law to the presiding court. In some jurisdictions, the parties are given an opportunity to object to any findings or conclusions before the "rented" judge's opinion is submitted to the presiding judge and entered as the judgment of the court.

There are criticisms of private judging. It is only available to those disputants who can afford to pay for it. Further, some say it removes the pressure from the court to practice legal reform and drains off judicial resources, i.e., judges can retire from the public bench and "ascend" to the private bench. Finally, similar to the shortcomings of arbitration, because the decisions are private, they may not be a matter of public record and offer no precedent. However, some statutory schemes provide for both filing a private judgment and appealing a private award to an appellate court.[3]

All of the processes discussed herein can be provided for in a contract or agreement that initially brings the parties together. Such a contract can merely provide that if a dispute arises, the parties will seek to resolve it through a private judge (or med-arb, or mini-trial, or any one of these processes). However, the better approach is to provide as much detail as possible, including the service to be used or the name of the private

---

2   Stephen B. Goldberg et al., Dispute Resolution: Negotiation, Mediation and Other Processes 428 (5th ed. 2007) (citations omitted).

3   For a more in-depth discussion of the pros and cons of private judging, see Richard Chernick, Private Judging, 3 BNA Alternative Dispute Resolution Report 397 (1989).

judge, the rules to be followed (e.g., the rules of practice of a named jurisdiction), and whether the decision will be binding.

There are various websites explaining the process and offering services. A review of them will demonstrate some differences in definitions.

Med-Arb

This process is a combination of mediation and arbitration, but it is placed under adjudicative methods because if the mediation does not bring the parties to a full agreement then the matter is arbitrated, and arbitration is adjudicative in nature. The process and its parameters arise out of an underlying contract between the parties. Its benefits include party control over facilitated negotiation (mediation), combined with the promise of ultimate finality and speed of arbitration. The parties agree ahead of time that if some or all issues are not resolved in mediation, they will proceed to arbitration. What can be problematic about this hybrid form is the continued use of the same neutral. The neutral has served in the mediation, hearing potentially confidential information from each party, and then if the parties fail to reach agreement in the mediation, the same neutral serves as an arbitrator, issuing a final and binding decision. A better approach is for the parties to first participate in mediation and if no agreement is reached, to submit to arbitration with a different person or panel serving as arbitrator. In the latter situation, the parties have participated in two separate, successive processes. In the former, the processes are merged and the same third-party neutral utilized. While med-arb may save time because the parties do not have to present their case twice, it can adversely impact on the appearance of neutrality of the third party.

> The participants may, in some circumstances, agree or contract for the mediator to decide the matter if they are unable to do so. . . . Using the informal, consensual process of mediation with no evidentiary or procedural rules as the basis for an imposed decision does, however, create a considerable risk that the more clever or sophisticated participant may distort or manipulate the mediation in order to influence the mediator's opinion.
>
> A combined process of mediation followed by arbitration, all performed by one person, has been used with some success in labor conflicts. This "med-arb" approach may work best when the participants are of relatively equal bargaining experience and the efficiency of a combined procedure outweighs the inhibiting or strategic effect of the mediator's anticipated role change.[4]

---

4   Jay Folberg & Alison Taylor, Mediation: A Comprehensive Guide to Resolving Conflicts Without Litigation 278 (1984).

Med-arb requires unusual skills on the part of the person who plays both roles. Mediators, after all, are retained to facilitate discussion and to help parties agree on their own solutions to problems. Arbitrators are retained to take evidence and to render a judgment following the parties' presentation of evidence. The dynamics of the two processes are substantially different: mediation strives to minimize the adversary nature of dispute, while arbitration works well within an adversary model. Because of its hybrid nature, med-arb seems most appropriate as a voluntary, private dispute resolution method with the parties having control over the choice of forum and the person or persons who serve as mediator-arbitrators.[5]

See Appendix C for an example. Martindale-Hubbell calls this Med-then-Arb. For other variations see *The Martindale-Hubbell ADR Primer*, http://www.martindale.com/pdf/med-arb.pdf.

There is also the relatively new process of Arb-Med (Arbitration-Mediation). As can be determined from the name, this hybrid process involves arbitrating first, with a binding award made upon the closing of the arbitration, but not disclosed to the parties. The parties then engage in mediation, in which they can reach their own agreement. If they are unable to do so, the arbitrator's award is made known and is binding.

Final-Offer Arbitration

In this unique form of arbitration, the neutral must choose between the final offer of each disputant. In other words, the arbitrator cannot make a compromise decision but rather must pick one of the party's final offers. For example, assume that the salary negotiations for a baseball player have reached a stalemate and that the owners and the player go to final-offer arbitration. The player is seeking an annual salary of $5 million and the owners are offering $2 million. While each might be willing to move from their position, closer to the other, they are afraid that if they do so the arbitrator may choose the salary midway between their respective offers. Therefore, if they stay at $2 million and $5 million, an arbitrator might choose $3.5 million as a compromise salary and make an award of that amount. But, if the owners, in an attempt at "good faith," move up to $3 million and the player does not change his offer, but remains at $5 million, the arbitrator might come in at $4 million. While this result will not necessarily occur, the possibility has a chilling effect on good-faith negotiations.

Final-offer arbitration was devised to force the parties to make more realistic offers so that the arbitrator, who must choose between the two, will choose the most realistic

---

5   Susan M. Leeson and Bryan M. Johnston, Ending It: Dispute Resolution in America 151 (1988).

offer. In the last example, the arbitrator would have to choose between $3 million and $5 million and, since the owners had made an effort toward compromise, might be likely to choose the $3 million figure.

This type of process has arisen to resolve conflicts where the parties are negotiating prospectively (over a future contract, rather than a past breach of contract) but cannot effectively abandon the negotiation or the contract.

> Although arbitration is frequently used to resolve disputes about the interpretation or application of an existing contract, it is rarely used to resolve disputes about what the terms of a new contract should be. The reasons for the reluctance to use arbitration in this context are manifold. Parties who have an unresolvable dispute as to their rights under an existing contract must find some adjudicative means to determine those rights, but parties who have an unresolvable dispute concerning what their rights should be under a contract they are seeking to negotiate typically are under no such obligation. If they cannot agree, each is free to seek other parties with whom to negotiate. Hence, they tend to be reluctant to vest a third party with the power to decide what their rights against each other should be. This reluctance is typically overcome only when negotiating parties are required, for any of a number of reasons, to deal exclusively with each other and to reach agreement.[6]

Final-offer arbitration is also used in the area of public sector collective bargaining, for example, between municipal employee unions and the municipality.

> Final-offer arbitration is...frequently used to resolve "interest" disputes in public-sector employment. In contrast to in major league baseball, however, public-sector "interest" arbitrators are frequently charged with determining a wide range of bargainable issues, in addition to salary all going to make up the terms of employment in the new agreement.
>
> In some states, the statutory scheme calls for each party to present to the arbitrators a "package" that includes a position on *all* the bargainable issues not yet agreed on. The arbitrators must then choose what they consider to be the more reasonable of the two "packages." In other states, in contrast, the arbitrators are allowed to consider each issue separately and to choose between the positions of the parties on an issue-by-issue basis. This variation enables them to develop their own compromise "package" by balancing the parties' positions on the various issues.[7]

---

6   Goldberg et al., *supra* note 2, at 304.

7   Scott R. Peppet, Alan Scott Rau, and Edward F. Sherman, Process of Dispute Resolution: The Role of Lawyers 937-938 (4th ed. 2006).

Court-Related Nonadjudicative Processes

Mini-Trial

Words sometimes catch the public imagination and take on a life of their own, and so it is with the "mini-trial." This term was attached by a New York Times story to a formal settlement device created in 1977 in connection with a corporate patent infringement dispute. It is not strictly speaking a trial at all, but a process that combines elements of adjudication with other processes such as negotiation and mediation.[8]

A mini-trial is particularly useful in resolving business disputes. It is a voluntary and private process of dispute resolution in which counsel for the parties are given the opportunity to present a summary of proofs and argument to an impartial third party who may have expertise in the area and who renders a decision based on the proofs presented. The presentation is made within an agreed-upon time frame and is made before top management representatives or individuals who have settlement authority. The parties may select the neutral, whose decision is not binding but, rather, is advisory and intended to assist the parties in reaching a mutually acceptable agreement. Sometimes the parties negotiate after the case is presented but before hearing the neutral's evaluation; sometimes they negotiate after.

This process is both structured and flexible. The structure comes from the history of the process itself, as well as from the procedural agreement that the parties sign when they enter into the mini-trial process. The flexibility comes from the parties' ability to design the process to meet their particular needs. It is private and, if successful, results in a contractually binding agreement.

> The concept underlying the mini-trial is that it provides each business executive with a crash course in the merits of the dispute — a brief, but firsthand view of the best case that can be put forward by the attorneys for both sides, supplemented, if necessary, by the views of a neutral. Armed with this information, as well as their knowledge of the business relationships of the parties, the executives are equipped to negotiate a resolution of their dispute that makes business sense.[9]

"The minitrial captured the imagination of corporate executives, at least in part because it put them rather than their lawyers in control of the outcome. . . . It turns

---

8 *Id.* at 543.

9 Goldberg et al., *supra* note 2, at 313.

legal disputes into business decisions."[10] In business disputes the process can take a variety of forms:

> [T]he companies involved may decide to use a neutral person simply as a referee, or they may ask for an opinion about how the case would fare in court. Or the parties may ask the person to become actively involved in mediating a resolution. Finally, the principals may decide to dispense with an outsider completely and preside over the minitrial themselves."[11]

Many lawyers like the mini-trial process because they still have the opportunity to use their repertoire of persuasive advocacy skills, which can be inhibited in mediation.

Some have called this process an "information exchange," rather than a mini-trial, because the former seems more descriptive. And it has its limitations. "A minitrial is not suitable for every case, particularly those with high emotional stakes and those that involve a legal issue for which the parties want an interpretation of a statute or a binding precedent. These cases may best be resolved in court."[12]

The American Arbitration Association offers the mini-trial as one of its processes and has developed procedures to facilitate its application. See http://www.adr.org/sp.asp?id=22007.

Summary Jury Trial

"The summary jury trial is an adaptation of the minitrial for cases in which the parties want more direct information about likely jury reaction than they would receive from the prediction of a minitrial neutral advisor."[13] This process is another form of abbreviated trial, with the addition of a jury. Counsel for each party makes a summary presentation of admissible evidence and arguments before a judge or other neutral and a six- or twelve-member jury. The jurors are drawn from the regular jury pool. They render an advisory (nonbinding) verdict.

Someone with decisionmaking authority from each party must be present to observe the presentation of evidence and the determination of the jury. This provides them with a realistic view of their position as they prepare for final settlement

---

10   Linda R. Singer, Settling Disputes: Conflict Resolution in Business, Families, and The Legal System 61 (2d ed. 1994).

11   *Id.* at 61.

12   Frank E.A. Sander, The Courthouse and Alternative Dispute Resolution *in* Negotiation Strategies for Mutual Gain: The Basic Seminar of the Program on Negotiation at Harvard Law School, Lavinia Hall ed., 56 (1993).

13   Goldberg et al., *supra* note 2, at 317.

negotiations. The attorneys are permitted to question the jurors regarding why and how they reached their decision. This inquiry aids the attorneys in further trial preparation but, more importantly, helps the parties see how a future jury might view their case.

The summary jury trial can be public or private, voluntary or involuntary (judge-ordered), and is nonbinding. Since it is still relatively costly and time-consuming, it is more likely to be used in large, complex cases that would require extended trial time.

If the matter is not settled as a result of the summary jury trial and ultimately has to go to trial, a different jury hears the case, although the same judge may or may not preside over the trial. The originator of this process, Judge Thomas Lambros of the U.S. District Court for the Northern District of Ohio, believes that the procedure should remain sufficiently flexible "to accommodate the needs and styles of its various users."[14]

Generally, the use of summary jury trials as a settlement technique is expanding across jurisdictional lines.

> Judge Enslen of the U.S. district court in Michigan used summary jury trials in two interesting cases. One was a complex waste dumping case with 93 claims. The plaintiff and the defendant each picked their best case and the judge picked one case in between. The three cases went to three different summary juries. Once these three *boundary* cases were settled, the outcomes and information were used to settle all the other 90 cases.
>
> Another interesting summary jury case involved a baby who was severely burned by very hot water. The plaintiff sued the manufacturer of the heater, claiming that the temperature valve was defective. The case was sent to a summary jury trial and the jury found for the defendant. When the parties spoke with the jury afterward, the jury told them that although the baby was terribly injured they did not think that the defendant was responsible. The jury, however, made it clear that if they had found liability, they would have awarded huge damages. The defendant's lawyer then told his client that although this jury did not find him liable one could not predict what another jury might do if the case were to be taken to court. He advised his client that it was his moral responsibility to give some money to the plaintiff; some would call this public relations. The defendant paid several hundred thousand dollars, the case was settled and did not go to court. This is another example of an imaginative resolution where both the defendant and the plaintiff were able to get most of what they wanted.[15]

---

14 Thomas Lambros, Summary Jury Trial — an Alternative Method of Resolving Disputes, 69 Judicature 286, 286-290 (1986).

15 Sander, *supra* note 12, at 56-57.

Focus Groups

A focus group is not so much an alternative dispute resolution process as it is another settlement technique. However, since law firms are using focus groups, it is important to be familiar with the concept. Like other settlement tools, a focus group can take many forms, but it is similar to a summary jury trial. The major difference is that it is done outside the courtroom and only one side of the litigation is present.

For example, party *A* sues party *B*. Trial is approaching and counsel for party *A* wants to get a better grasp on how a jury might view his case. This can be accomplished by presenting a shortened version of the trial to a jury that is paid to sit and listen to the trial and reach a verdict like any other jury. However, instead of party *B* and their lawyers participating, someone from party *A*'s firm role-plays party *B*'s part. The jury hears both sides of the case, reaches a verdict, and can then be questioned by counsel as to why they reached that verdict. The jury can also be divided before deliberations and return two separate verdicts, sometimes diametrically opposed.

A focus group is considered a settlement tool because, as it gives the law firm and the client a more realistic view of their case and their chances in court, it can frequently lead to a reasonable early settlement.

Neutral Expert Factfinding

This process of dispute resolution uses a neutral third party to make recommendations based upon her expertise. The *expertise* of the neutral is the most important aspect here. The process can take on a variety of forms. It can be voluntary (generally private and outside the judicial system) or involuntary (court-ordered), and is nonbinding. The expert, however, may submit her findings to the judge.

The precise form the process takes seems to depend on its origination. "Early neutral evaluation" is court-ordered and

> calls for assessment of the case early in its history by an experienced neutral (usually a volunteer attorney selected by the court) on the basis of brief presentations by both sides. If the case does not settle, the assessment is kept confidential, and the evaluator helps the parties to simplify and tailor the case for more expeditious handling in trial. Sometimes the evaluator also assists the parties in monitoring discovery requests.[16]

> When business disagreements result from differing views of critical scientific, technical, business, or even legal information, the parties may be able to negotiate their own settlement, with or without a mediator, if they can resolve their

16 Goldberg et al., *supra* note 2, at 318.

conflicting perceptions. What they often need is an outside expert, whose knowledge and impartiality they all respect, to give an unbiased opinion.[17]

Furthermore, "[i]n complicated disagreements over faulty construction, medical malpractice, personal injuries, patent and securities regulation, and antitrust violations, neutral experts can help disputants to understand what is at issue and to make informed decisions concerning their liability.[18]

Sometimes "the expert may mediate, though more often [he] simply provides the parties with an impartial opinion of the facts or applicable standards or a prediction of which party would be found at fault in a trial or administrative proceeding."[19] The proceeding is more investigatory and informal rather than tied to the rules of evidence. Finally, the procedure, as used in this context, is generally private.

Factfinding may be just one stage of the dispute resolution process in this field. It may be followed by mediation, arbitration, or litigation.

Early Settlement/Bar Paneling

In this process, which takes place within the court structure, attorneys, with or without their clients present, meet with a panel of volunteer attorneys who hear a summary of the case and make suggestions regarding settlement. If the clients are not present at the discussions, the attorneys take the panel's suggestions back to them. The expertise and authority of the panel depends on their being familiar with practice in the pertinent subject matter as well as geographic area. The panel can therefore be relied on to predict, with some degree of accuracy, the outcome of a judicial hearing. Bar paneling frequently occurs in subject matter specialties, such as matrimonial law or medical malpractice.

Noncourt-Related Nonadjudicative Processes

Ombudsperson

The use of an ombudsperson is a private, voluntary, and investigatory process in which an individual (the ombudsperson) hears disputes or complaints and sometimes makes recommendations as to how to resolve them. The ombudsperson

---

17 Singer, *supra* note 10, at 65.

18 *Id.* at 69.

19 *Id.* at 25.

may investigate complaints from within the organization, as well as complaints against it by consumers, for example. The services of an ombudsperson are used by corporations, educational institutions, hospitals, and similar entities having a large or complicated organization. An ombudsperson is usually an employee of the corporation or institution, but may also be an outsider. Making this service available represents an attempt by the organization to provide a system to deal with employee, patient, or customer complaints. Initially, the ombudsperson may serve as a mediator. If that is not successful, the ombudsperson may make a recommendation as to how the dispute should be resolved, which is generally nonbinding. The process is of an informal nature.

One expert has defined an ombudsperson as

> a neutral or impartial manager within a corporation, who may provide confidential and informal assistance to managers and employees in resolving work-related concerns, who may serve as a counselor, go-between, mediator, fact-finder or upward-feedback mechanism, and whose office is located outside ordinary line management structures. . . . In technical terminology, the ombudsman is committed to integrative solutions, and avoids distributive solutions both by the design of the office (an informal, nonadjudicatory structure) and by personal commitment. . . . Most ombuds practitioners report to the CEO or someone close to the CEO.[20]

Another expert has observed:

> Most U.S. ombudspeople work for the organizations they monitor. Yet they remain outside of the ordinary chains of command and generally report to the chief executive officer of a company or agency. . . . In explaining how they can be neutral when they work for the employer who is part of a dispute, these people say that their job is to assure employees of fair process and that their loyalty to the employer is satisfied when they settle disputes among employees evenhandedly. . . . Some ombudspeople believe that their additional role of undertaking independent investigations and recommending changes to management, gives them more visibility and clout than in-house mediators have and helps to compensate for the possible effect on their credibility of the fact that they are insiders.[21]

---

20 Mary P. Rowe, The Corporate Ombudsman: An Overview and Analysis, *in* Negotiation Theory and Practice 433-434 (J. William Breslin & Jeffrey Z. Rubin eds., 1993).

21 Singer, *supra* note 10, at 25-26, 100, 101-102.

One ombudsperson[22] lists the principal functions of an ombudsman as follows:

1. Dealing with feelings

2. Giving and receiving information on a one-to-one basis[23]

3. Counseling and problem-solving to help the manager or employee help himself or herself

4. Shuttle diplomacy

5. Mediation

6. Investigation

7. Adjudication or arbitration (rare)

8. Upward feedback[24]

In discussing what types of problems come to an ombudsperson to handle, she includes the following:

> salary and benefits; promotion and demotion; performance appraisals; job security and retirement issues; company policies; discipline/termination; discrimination and harassment; safety, ethics and whistleblowing; transfers; personality conflicts/meanness; information/referral; suggestions; working conditions; personal health, mentoring, and counseling issues; management practices; bizarre behavior and problems.[25]

Ombudspeople hail from a variety of backgrounds, including human resources, legal, technical, and managerial roles. As in many dispute resolution processes, the role played by the ombudsperson varies with each setting. However, its flexibility and value make it a viable profession in dispute resolution.

---

22 Rowe, *supra* note 20, at 436-438.

23 "[A]n ombudsman is likely to be the bellwether or early warning device for whatever problems the employer has not yet met, but will soon have to deal with. Examples of such problems include sexual harassment in the early 1970s, AIDS in the early 1980s, and now new kinds of drug problems." *Id.* at 436.

24 "Possibly the most important function of the ombudsman is to receive, perhaps analyze, then pass along information that will foster timely change in a company." *Id.* at 438.

25 *Id.* at 441.

There are a number of professional ombudsman associations and sections, including:

- The United States Ombudsman Association (serving governmental ombudsman offices). *http://www.usombudsman.org.*

- The International Ombudsman Association (advances the profession of organizational ombudsman). *http://www.ombudsassociation.org.*

- The Ombudsman Section of the Association for Conflict Resolution (professional organization). *http://www.mediate.com/acrombuds.*

It should be noted that the ombuds concept originated in Sweden, but has experienced significant growth in the United States and elsewhere.

Conciliation

The *Dictionary of Conflict Resolution* at page 102, defines "conciliation" as "the act of bringing together; attempt, usually by a third party who may or may not be neutral, to encourage the parties to settle their dispute." Conciliation occurs when a third-party neutral gathers disputants at a meeting to discuss their conflicts.

While some consider conciliation to be synonymous with meditation, it is not. Conciliation is usually limited to getting the parties to communicate, either face-to-face or through other measures. The conciliator does not necessarily participate in that communication. "Unlike mediation, conciliation, or convening, usually connotes only preliminary involvement by a third party. The outsider may bring the parties together or carry a few messages back and forth.[26] Mediation, on the other hand, is usually face-to-face, and the mediator facilitates the active communication of the parties in an attempt to resolve their differences.

Conciliation as a form of dispute resolution is most often found in an international context.

Facilitation

Facilitation is a collaborative process that involves a group of people trying to resolve differences or strategize or plan for future endeavors. The facilitator uses a variety of techniques to enhance, organize, and direct communication so that the group may move forward, either out of the conflict or toward a particular goal. "Facilitators may act as moderators in large meetings, making sure that everyone is able to speak and be heard. Facilitators are not expected to volunteer their own ideas or

---

26 Singer, *supra* note 10, at 24.

participate actively in moving parties toward agreement."[27] Facilitators may do extensive preliminary work in meeting with various subgroups to develop an agenda and focus the subgroups. Generally, the facilitator does not have a stake in the outcome of the group endeavor, but rather has an interest in the success of the process itself. It is most frequently used in the areas of public policy and international trade, but can be applied in any area where a divergence of views is brought to a group meeting. Some see it more as conflict prevention, rather than conflict resolution.

Summary

There are a number of variations on the themes of negotiation, mediation, and arbitration. Some are used only in particular settings and others are used sparingly, but in a broader range of applications.

The adjudicative processes are private judging, med-arb, arb-med, and final-offer arbitration. These are all private and the parties pay the neutral's fees. All are subject to process criticism, as well as to the parties' affirmation. *Private judging* arises through the consent of the parties or direction of the court. The latter occurs in complex matters with trial pending. In some states, decisions are filed with the court and are subject to appeal; in others they are not, depending upon statute. *Med-arb* is a creature of contract. It is a combination of mediation first, followed by arbitration if the parties cannot agree in mediation. The neutral may be the same or a different person. In *arb-med* the process is reversed. An award is private and is treated the same as other arbitration awards. *Final-offer arbitration* is used largely in public employee interest and baseball player salary disputes. Each party submits a final offer and the neutral must select one of the offers. The results may be made public because of citizen interest.

There are also nonadjudicative processes. These can be further subdivided into those relating to litigation and those that are not litigation inspired. They can be private or court annexed. The first five — mini-trial, summary jury trial, focus groups, neutral expert factfinding, and early settlement/bar paneling — are considered "settlement techniques" intended to get the parties to objectively view their case and consider the benefits of settlement.

Both the *mini-trial* and *summary jury trial* are abbreviated versions of a trial, presented by counsel before a neutral and before the parties or their representatives who have decisionmaking authority. Summary jury trial is before a jury, whose members can be questioned about the verdict. After the trial, the parties negotiate toward settlement with the added advantage of having seen a summary of their case tried.

---

27   *Ibid.*

The use of *focus groups* to serve as jurors is similar to the summary jury trial, except (1) only one side of the litigation is responsible for the mock trial, (2) it is done privately outside the court system, and (3) the jurors are paid.

When a neutral is brought in as an *expert,* his role is to hear the case and help the parties agree on technical disputes that may require the input of an expert. The expert also makes nonbinding recommendations. *Bar paneling* uses the good offices of volunteer attorneys who hear abbreviated presentations of the case from counsel and then help settlement negotiations through suggestions based on their expertise and knowledge of the court.

Noncourt-related, nonadjudicative processes include the role of *ombudsperson, conciliator,* and *facilitator.* The former is usually an employee of a corporation or institution who hears conflicts within the organization or conflicts between the organization and others, i.e., customers. In this role, the ombudsperson serves as an investigator, mediator, teacher, and diplomat, attempting to resolve conflict and keep the employer informed about problems, without involving the employer in the particular problem. A conciliator, on the other hand, is a neutral who brings the disputing parties together to discuss their differences, but may not necessarily participate in those discussions. A *facilitator* works with *groups* to guide and enhance their discussions to work through a dispute or plan for a future endeavor.

EXERCISES

1. Research your state court to determine which of the processes described in this chapter are being used within the court system, either court annexed or court referred.

2. Do the same research as above, but with reference to private dispute resolution applications available.

3. Develop a chart based on the foregoing research that indicates what processes are being used, where they are being used, and, finally, for what types of disputes (labor, contract, family, medical malpractice, etc.).

4. Observe and report on one of the processes being used to resolve an actual conflict.

5. Develop several hypothetical conflicts in which you would use one of the processes described in this chapter. In a class discussion, ask other students which process they would apply. Discuss which process is most appropriate and why.

6. Do research using one of the dispute resolution journals regarding an ethical or policy issue in one of the processes discussed in this chapter.

7. Interview a neutral who has participated in these processes and ask him or her to compare several of the ADR processes.

8. Develop a role play for students in the class to act out and apply one of the processes.

9. Determine whether your college or university has an ombudsperson and interview him or her about his or her responsibilities and professional background.

Med-Arb Role Play

Retail Clothing

After lengthy negotiations, Global Fashion, a large retail store, has entered into a five-year agreement with Nguyen Enterprises, a Vietnamese clothing manufacturer, for the purchase and sale of a mid-priced line of women's and girls clothing, to be sold in Global Fashion's stores commencing in three months. Minimum orders and timelines have been established. The parties believed that prices had also been established, but later events indicate a confusion or misunderstanding about cost. There is also disagreement about marketing, which was not addressed in the contract.

The contract between the parties indicates that if a disagreement arises under the contract, the parties will first seek the assistance of a mediator. If mediation does not resolve the conflict, then the parties will move to arbitration, with a different neutral. The parties also disagree about who should be the provider of these services and you have been asked to recommend at least three providers for them to choose from. One company/organization should provide both services. Finally, there is a question about whether the issue of marketing is even subject to a dispute resolution, since it was not included in the original contract.

Policy, Ethical, and Practice Issues

7

Standard V: Confidentiality
Standard VI: Quality of the Process
Standard VII: Advertising and Solicitation
Standard VIII: Fees and Other Charges
Standard IX: Advancement of Mediation Practice

Arbitration Ethics

Summary

Exercises

Introduction

As in any field of endeavor, issues of policy, ethics, education, and application are debated among the practitioners, policymakers, and academics. These debates contribute to the molding of the future of the field. They also reflect the vitality and growth of the profession.

This chapter presents current thinking on *some* of these issues and encourages the student to research others and to keep abreast of emerging questions and debates in the discipline. Thoughtful, critical consideration of policy and professional issues contributes to the development of each student's ethical self.

In reviewing these materials, one will find that there is some necessary overlap among the policy, ethical, and practice issues. How they are distinguished will depend on the perspective adopted. Some issues are policy considerations, to be made by program developers in conjunction with providers and clients; others are ethical issues for individual mediators (but are affected by policy decisions); and one is a practice issue (but could be included in policy decisions).

Policy Issues

Institutionalizing ADR Systems Within the Court System

While some jurisdictions may still question the efficacy of institutionalizing ADR systems within the court, the current focus is more on the manner in which and the extent to which such institutionalization occurs. There are many ways to connect the two, from processes provided within the court by court personnel, to court-referred programs, from voluntary programs to mandated ones.

Some court systems that were at the forefront of the movement to institutionalize ADR within the court are now considering how to achieve a *comprehensive* dispute resolution system. In such a system, more options are available to disputants and ADR is better woven into the fabric of the court system; disputants are better educated regarding their choices in ADR and litigation, and are empowered to choose the process that best suits their particular situation.

Looking at the larger picture in his online article about the Florida court system, Gregory Firestone explains: "Providing parties with multiple dispute resolution options and encouraging them to select the process that most suits their case appears to lead to greater party satisfaction and improves the chances for resolution. Educating parties about the options and providing opportunities for parties to 'loop back' to new ADR methods when one method fails also increases the chances that ADR options will be successful prior to litigation."[1] He also suggests that ultimately the system may emerge wherein litigation may be one of the dispute resolution options, rather than the entry point into the court system.

A related issue questions which mediation model should be used within the court system: evaluative, facilitative, or transformative. That choice can have an effect on litigants' experience with mediation, as well as the dominance of a particular model. It also impacts the following mandatory or voluntary participation by litigants.

Mandatory vs. Voluntary Participation in ADR Within the Court System

This is a subissue of the foregoing. As courts and bar associations integrate ADR, we see the mandating of some ADR systems. A point of clarification here: "Mandates to participate in a dispute resolution process should be distinguished from coercion to settle once participation has begun."[2] "Mandatory" is applied to those processes in which "the third-party neutral lacks authority to issue a binding decision, such as mediation, conciliation, early neutral evaluation, moderated settlement conferences, and summary jury trials, and with processes in which parties can reject the award and assert the right to trial, such as court-annexed arbitration."[3]

---

1   Gregory Firestone, Court ADR Systems: The Road Ahead (2007), *http://www.mediate.com*, original in ACResolution, Vol. 6, Issue 1.

2   Mandated Participation and Settlement Coercion: Dispute Resolution as It Relates to the Courts, Report #1 of the Law and Public Policy Committee of the Society of Professionals in Dispute Resolution, Washington, D.C. (1991), at 6.

3   *Ibid.*

The resulting case appears to be that in mediation, a disputant, if participating in "mandatory mediation," is only compelled to be informed about the process. In other forms of ADR within the court, when participation is mandated, the result is not binding, unless the parties agree to enter into a binding contract thereafter.

The "Dark Side" of ADR

ADR has its critics. They believe that processes that keep disputes and their resolution private harm the public. In certain situations, that is true. An example would be if a company harms an individual with a new product but resolves the resulting personal injury lawsuit privately, the product could conceivably continue to harm other consumers. Likewise, charges of pollution that are mediated without all the necessary parties present can result in harm to those not present. However, in considering this argument, we must keep in mind that even when parties litigate, they can settle their litigation and keep the terms of the settlement private.

Another criticism is that because of private settlement, some of the legal reform and development that comes about through judicial decisions is lost. Suppose, for example, that the legal issues surrounding a person's right to die or a surrogate parent's right to keep her child were not decided in the courts and not brought to public attention. The public would have no guideposts for behavior in those situations in the absence of judicial decision or legislative fiat.

Similarly, there is concern about those disputants who are less powerful in comparison to the other party so that, without protection, they will suffer. The stronger party is able to intimidate, harass, and generally impose their will on the other. If representatives (such as attorneys or other advocates) are not present to protect the powerless, and the neutral is unable or unwilling, due to other constraints, to protect them,[4] has the legal community put such weaker parties in jeopardy by permitting ADR to deal with their conflict? One response to this criticism is that the court is not always effective in dealing with such power imbalances. For example, a powerful corporation has the financial ability to hire the brightest and best legal counsel and has the time to delay litigation in defense against a poor consumer who cannot afford an hourly legal bill sufficient to properly deal with the corporate defendant. Nor can the consumer wait out the delaying tactics.

Let us look at one more criticism of ADR, particularly court-mandated ADR. In many instances, it imposes another step in the legal process. This results in additional

---

4   The neutral may be unwilling to intervene because of the commitment to impartiality. See *infra* at page 143.

delays, lost time from work, and frustration for the parties. Entire classes of cases — for example, all damage cases under a certain dollar amount — are sent to arbitration. The parties appear, present their case, and the arbitrator makes an award. If the parties are dissatisfied with the award, they must so notify the court and come back for a trial de novo. This is frequently done in the "less significant" cases, thereby creating a "second class" justice system. Even those who strongly support ADR and its use cannot deny this problem exists and requires attention.

Another area where mediation is utilized, and where problems or misuse may arise, is school-based peer mediation. Some educators believe that peer mediation can be utilized to address a bullying issue between two students. However, many others in the field disagree. In a bullying situation there is a terrible power imbalance, similar to spousal abuse; the bully or abuser is much more powerful and has intimidated and repeatedly attacked the target. The process of mediation requires a greater level of power equity in order to function and provide a fair and safe outcome, and is therefore inappropriate in the bullying context.

This discussion does not exhaust the criticisms that have been leveled at ADR. Rather it is meant to raise issues, alert the student, and aid in the student's critical analysis of the field.

To Regulate or Not to Regulate?

State regulation of ADR providers, particularly private mediators, is a topic of interest. Those in favor of regulation cite the need to protect uninformed consumers from unscrupulous or untrained mediators, the absence of professional self-regulation, and the lack of consistency in the background and training of existing private providers. Providers of court-annexed mediation generally have to meet certain minimum standards in training and/or experience and/or education background. The standards are higher for providers of family/custody mediation within the court system.

Certain professional groups, such as the Association for Conflict Resolution and the Academy of Family Mediators, for example, publish professional standards. And although few states license private ADR providers at this time, some states and organizations do have a mediator certification or roster system in place. The problem with setting standards, however, is that it is difficult to clearly measure the diverse attributes of competent ADR providers, which include maturity, sensitivity, education, subject matter expertise, and well-developed communication skills.

It remains incumbent upon professional organizations and dispute resolution providers to maintain high standards of service and education to avoid public criticism. Further, the profession has a responsibility to educate the public regarding provider training and standards of professional conduct.

How Is Success Measured?

Court-annexed ADR has been touted as relieving court congestion, saving money, and providing a more informal process for the disputant. Has it done this and should it do this? In developing a program, the initiators must first determine what they are trying to accomplish and why. For example, are they looking to increase the public's satisfaction with the legal process or are they looking to reduce the court's expenditures and ease court congestion? Are they looking to avoid the need to appoint more judges? Their reasons may be all of these and more. However, they need to be clear on their goals. Only then can a system be properly developed to meet their goals and studied to determine if the goals have been met.

If the system of ADR that is developed meets the goals, then it is successful. If it does not, then one must determine whether it satisfies other goals or should be eliminated in whole or in part. It is not sufficient to say ADR is a good thing and everyone else is doing it and, therefore, we want to do it too.

This issue is raised in another context, particularly in mediation. If the court, or the funding source in community mediation, determines success by number of cases that reach settlement within the shortest period of time, a great disservice has been done to all involved. Effective mediation takes time — to hear the parties, to permit them to vent anger and frustration if necessary, to enable them to develop their own resolution, and to learn to work with each other. A mediator who is being judged by the number of cases settled will most likely be more intrusive and controlling in the mediation and less likely to adequately listen to the parties and their needs.

Further, settlement can occur after the mediation process is abandoned because the parties were at least given the opportunity to hear each other. Thus, even when matters are not resolved, parties have expressed satisfaction with the process. Perhaps some parties feel listened to and empowered. Perhaps some disputants learn to communicate better as a result of the mediation. The value of mediation is very difficult to measure and imposing unreasonable time constraints limits its viability as an effective process.

Considering the length of time a case may take to mediate, particularly a community matter where the parties have an ongoing relationship, some critics of ADR point to the fact that it would take less time in court. However, they are not looking at the larger picture. Is the court better able to deal with the disputants in such a way as to dissuade their return to court on another matter. Does the court deal with the underlying interpersonal conflict that can erupt later with another "cause"? In mediation, the parties may come to a better understanding of each other, may learn to communicate better with each other, or may decide that they do not like each other and have no wish to continue a relationship. Whatever the result, the parties have decided the outcome, not the court; this alone empowers the parties.

Policy/Ethical Issues

Some concerns in the field of dispute resolution have both a policy impact on the planners and developers of an ADR program, as well as an ethical impact on the individual practitioners. We have already considered the example of how a mediator must face time constraints or be expected to reach a "success quota of settlements" while at the same time trying to adequately mediate a lengthy, involved, and heated conflict that will take substantially more time than he can afford to give. Without the beneficial settlement statistics, the ADR program might lose funding; but without time spent on this particular case, it will not be resolved, or the resolution will not "stick" because all the issues have not been dealt with. Therefore, it is incumbent upon developers of programs to not let settlement statistics "run the program."

This section considers similar policy/ethical issues.

Is ADR Appropriate in All Types of Cases?

This is another issue in which there are strongly held beliefs on both sides. Here we consider but two examples of the debate.

Domestic Violence

Most people who work in the area of domestic violence strongly oppose the use of mediation; some even go so far as to advocate that it be categorically rejected. First, however, in any particular case, one must look more critically at the issues involved.

Is there a history of domestic violence between the couple, or one incident? A history of violence puts the dispute and its resolution in a different category. It is likely that there is a severe power imbalance and that the victim is terrified of the abuser and has a very diminished capacity to negotiate on her own behalf. Where this is true, mediation probably is inappropriate. If there has been only a single, relatively minor incident of domestic violence, and the parties appear to be able to confront each other and deal with each other, then mediation may be appropriate and beneficial.

Determining the frequency of domestic violence, or its effects on the parties, can prove to be very difficult for the mediator or for those who are screening the cases. And some legal professionals will raise a further question: Is there merely an allegation of domestic violence to gain an advantage in litigation, or is it real? This is also difficult to determine and may be beyond the mediator's abilities.

Related to the issue of the existence of domestic violence or its frequency is the general question of whether or not these cases *can be* screened out of mediation. Most people are ashamed of domestic violence in their families and will not openly admit its occurrence. Therefore, the mediator may not even be aware of domestic violence or may first become aware of it during the mediation.

What is being mediated — parenting arrangements, financial issues, or the continuance of the relationship (and, therefore, the violence itself)? Most people maintain that the violence itself cannot be mediated. The answer to whether other issues can be mediated when domestic violence has occurred may go back to the question of whether there is too great a power imbalance between the parties.

> Mediation . . . places the parties on equal footing and asks them to negotiate an agreement for future behavior. Beyond failing to punish assailants for their crimes, this process implies that victims share responsibility for the illegal conduct and requires them to modify their own behavior in exchange for the assailants' promises not to commit further crimes.[5]

Mediation of the violent acts is clearly a subversion of the law and a violation of the victim, which cannot be tolerated.

Does this mean that mediation simply cannot work in cases of domestic violence? Some say yes. But those who support continued attempts at mediation where domestic violence has occurred say no. The latter individuals point to ongoing violence in our society and throughout the world and hold up mediation as one possible solution that must continue to be available and that has the potential to transform the parties.

By removing all domestic violence cases from mediation, is the ADR community giving up on self-determination and transformation through mediation? This is less a practice issue and more a philosophical one. One of the reasons mediation is so powerful is that it gives the dispute and its resolution back to the parties. It empowers them to reach their own resolution of the conflict. It demonstrates to them the skills necessary to deal with future conflicts. However, parties must be ready and open to such benefits, and victims and perpetrators of domestic violence are not likely to possess that openness. One proposal is to not mandate mediation in cases of domestic violence, but to permit the parties — with knowledge of the process, advice of counsel, and support of therapy — to request mediation. This, of course, excludes those who do not have the necessary financial or experiential resources.

---

5   Lisa G. Lerman, Mediation of Wife Abuse Cases: The Adverse Impact of Informal Dispute Resolution on Women, 7 Harv. Women's L.J. 57, 72 (1984), *quoting* United States Commission on Civil Rights, under the Rule of Thumb: Battered Women and the Administration of Justice 1 (1982).

The ACR's Standards of Practice for Family and Divorce Mediation, in Standard X states:

> A family mediator shall recognize a family situation involving domestic abuse and take appropriate steps to shape the mediation process accordingly.
>
> A. As used in these Standards, domestic abuse includes domestic violence as defined by applicable state law and issues of control and intimidation.
> B. A mediator shall not undertake a mediation in which the family situation has been assessed to involve domestic abuse without appropriate and adequate training.
> C. Some cases are not suitable for mediation because of safety, control or intimidation issues. A mediator should make a reasonable effort to screen for the existence of domestic abuse prior to entering into an agreement to mediate. The mediator should continue to assess for domestic abuse throughout the mediation process.
> D. If domestic abuse appears to be present the mediator shall consider taking measures to insure the safety of participants and the mediator including, among others:
>   1. establishing appropriate security arrangements;
>   2. holding separate sessions with the participants even without the agreement of all participants;
>   3. allowing a friend, representative, advocate, counsel or attorney to attend the mediation sessions;
>   4. encouraging the participants to be represented by an attorney, counsel or an advocate throughout the mediation process;
>   5. referring the participants to appropriate community resources;
>   6. suspending or terminating the mediation sessions, with appropriate steps to protect the safety of the participants.
> E. The mediator should facilitate the participants' formulation of parenting plans that protect the physical safety and psychological well-being of themselves and their children.[6]

Sexual Harassment Grievances

Related in concept to the issue of domestic violence, but not in application, is the question of whether sexual harassment grievances in the workplace should be

6   http://www.ACRnet.org/acrlibrary/more.php?id=P36_0_1_0_C.

submitted to mediation prior to going to arbitration. Once again, one must approach with caution. One professional maintains that

> sexual harassment cases are similar in power structure to domestic violence or criminal assault matters. In those cases there is more than a simple dispute over money or property. Instead, there is a dynamic present that involves power, fear, and coercion. These elements underlie the "dispute" being mediated. . . . But like an iceberg, only the tip is visible, and the most dangerous part remains unseen. In those situations, there is an imbalance of power between the batterer and the victim that cannot be reconciled in mediation. Many legal commentators have concluded that mediation is inappropriate in these cases unless special circumstances are present. Because the same dynamic exists between harasser and victim, mediation is also inappropriate in sexual harassment grievance cases.[7]

Similar to the question of whether mediation "covers up" the crime of spousal abuse when it is used to resolve cases of domestic violence, there is concern that the actions of a harasser in the workplace will go unpunished in mediation. "Grievance mediation of these cases, no matter how well intended, risks trivializing the seriousness of sexual harassment and maintaining an inhospitable environment for the female workforce."[8]

Of equal importance is the process of clearly defining the behavior that constitutes sexual harassment. Lack of definition creates uncertainty about what kind of behavior is acceptable. Such a definition cannot continue to be refined through case law if the behavior is mediated and therefore does not come before the court or the public. Sexual harassment cases that are "settled" may send the wrong message to other employees. Victims may believe that future claims will not be taken seriously and harassers may believe that unacceptable behavior will go unpunished.

The decision to mediate sexual harassment cases cannot be made on a case-by-case basis because it is usually provided for in the employment contract. Therefore, mediation in such a case must be closely monitored as to its effectiveness.

> For mediation to be accepted as an alternative to an adjudicatory process, such as grievance arbitration, the mediator must be fair, impartial, and nonjudgmental;

---

7 Mori Irvine, Mediation: Is It Appropriate for Sexual Harassment Grievances?, 9 Ohio St. J. Dis. Resol. 28 (1993).

8 *Id.* at 28.

the process must be voluntary and free of bias; and the parties must be equals in the dispute. . . . [A]dherence to this criteria is crucial for the process to be considered appropriate and legitimate.[9]

ADR policymakers need to study the appropriateness of a particular process to a particular class of cases or disputes. Not all divorce cases should be mediated — some are being arbitrated and some still need to go to trial. Perhaps one should consider a mini-trial for divorce matters. Not all business dissolutions should be arbitrated. Some should be mediated, or use a neutral expert. Not all personal injury cases should be arbitrated. Some require the gentler hand of mediation and others perhaps need the input of a summary jury trial. We need to look at the attributes of particular cases to determine the appropriateness of each process. It is important to keep open minds on this issue and not classify and categorize disputes by which ADR process is used to resolve them.

Qualification of Neutrals

A principal issue regarding the qualification of neutrals is whether the neutral needs process training. Most professionals would say there should be a requirement of at least *some* minimal training to qualify the arbitrator, mediator, or other neutral. If a neutral does not know what a mediator, for example, does and the tools he uses to do it, the neutral might end up serving as an expert factfinder instead of a mediator.

Training can be provided by the court system, an organizational provider, undergraduate or graduate school, law school, or through a variety of other training sources. Most training provides for simulations or role plays to give the student an opportunity to practice the newly learned techniques. In some programs, particularly in the law school setting, students are given the opportunity, through clinics, to serve as neutrals and to counsel clients through an ADR process. While there may be some "natural" mediators out there, just like there are some "natural" teachers, both require training.

Is it necessary for a neutral to be schooled in the theory and/or law of the process in which she serves? Not necessarily, but that education does provide the practitioner with a more well-developed background in the process. It acts in a way similar to experience. A mediator who has significant experience, and has thought reflectively and critically about that experience, is a more mature professional. Similarly, a mediator who has studied the mediation process from an academic perspective and participated

---

9 *Id.* at 32.

in ethical and policy discussions in addition to having the training previously mentioned is a more well-rounded professional. Neither necessarily makes the neutral better, but perhaps richer.

Should the neutral have subject matter knowledge? Should, for example, someone who arbitrates the breakup of a professional corporation whose main asset is real estate, which must be valued, have experience in or knowledge about real estate valuation? This is a complex question which divides the experts. Some professionals maintain that an expert in the *process,* particularly mediation, has sufficient knowledge to serve. In fact, the absence of substantive knowledge is a benefit because the neutral will not be tempted to prejudge (in arbitration) or offer options (in mediation). Others say that in some complex areas — such as environmental, medical, or domestic relations — subject matter knowledge is either helpful or essential. Finally, there are those who maintain that subject matter knowledge is essential for *all* neutrals.

How one answers the question about the need for subject matter knowledge may depend on the ADR process being considered and the nature of the conflict. Arbitrators, for example, may be expected to have, and frequently are chosen, for their subject matter expertise.

Ethical Issues

Ethical dilemmas are not uncommon to practitioners of ADR. Those faced by mediators can be addressed through the Model Standards of Conduct for Mediators promulgated by the American Arbitration Association, the American Bar Association, and the Association for Conflict Resolution. The most recent edition is dated September 2005, and the full text is in Appendix A. It addresses Self Determination, Impartiality, Conflict of Interest, Competence, Confidentiality, Quality of the Process, Advertising and Solicitation, Fees and Other Charges, and finally Advancement of Mediation Practice.

Standard I: Self-Determination

The parties' self-determination is the cornerstone of mediation and it can be lost or impaired by an overly directive or controlling mediator. "A mediator shall respect and encourage self-determination by the parties in their decision whether, and on what terms, to resolve their dispute, and shall refrain from being directive and judgmental regarding the issues in dispute and options for settlement."[10]

---

10   Robert A. Baruch Bush, The Dilemmas of Mediation Practice: A Study of Ethical Dilemmas and Policy Implications, 35 (1992).

Standard II: Impartiality

"Impartiality means absence of favoritism or bias — i.e., expressed sympathy or antipathy — toward any party or any position taken by a party to a mediation. In addition, it means a commitment to aid all parties, as opposed to a single party, in exploring the possibilities for resolution."[11] This applies to both verbal and non-verbal communications and actions. It often happens in an ADR setting that one party is offensive, aggressive, or intemperate while the other is quiet, less powerful, or needful of protection. The natural reaction is to try to help the party in need of protection. However, as this can interfere with the parties' self-determination and autonomy, it is essential that the neutral remain unbiased.

Where the neutral's impartiality is in question, she should decline to serve, offer to withdraw, or withdraw from serving.[12]

Standard III: Conflict of Interest

Any neutral must avoid a conflict of interest, which is generally described as the neutral's having some business or personal connection with one of the parties or their representative. The parties must be informed and given the opportunity to seek another neutral. A more subtle problem can arise when the neutral develops a relationship with one of the parties or their representative after the process. Is the neutral prohibited from entering into such a relationship out of concern that the other party may become aware of it and believe that it predated the process and compromises the neutral's objectivity? The neutral must avoid both the appearance and the reality of a conflict.

Standard IV: Competence

A neutral should not accept a case in which he feels he does not possess the experience or substantive knowledge necessary to serve the disputants. Similarly, if a neutral accepts a case and thereafter determines that he does not have the sufficient knowledge to proceed, he has the responsibility to withdraw. In both situations, the neutral should inform the parties as to his limits. Finally, it is the neutral's responsibility to "obtain necessary skills and substantive training appropriate to his/her areas of practice, and to upgrade those skills on an ongoing basis."[13]

---

11   *Id.* at 34.

12   *Ibid.*

13   *Ibid.*

Standard V: Confidentiality

"Maintaining confidentiality is critical to the dispute resolution process. Confidentiality encourages candor, a full exploration of the issues and a neutral's acceptability."[14] The duty to maintain confidentiality extends to third parties not present at the mediation, such as attorneys, the courts, and referring agencies, as well as between the disputants. The mediator must keep confidential all things disclosed in caucus, unless the speaker consents to disclosure. This duty to maintain confidentiality is limited only by statutory requirements of disclosure.

The appropriate level of confidentiality that is required depends on the ADR process, its source, the preference of the parties, and any contractual provisions.

Standard VI: Quality of the Process

This is a broad, overarching standard including diligence, timeliness, safety, appropriate parties, their participation and competency, fairness, and respect. It also addresses domestic abuse or violence among the parties.

The neutral has the duty to uphold the integrity of the process. Part of that duty includes staying within the bounds of the neutral's role. For example, a mediator who is a lawyer should not give legal advice, or, if a counselor, he should not counsel the parties. Neither of these is within the role of mediator.

A further part of this responsibility to maintain the quality of the process is to encourage other neutrals, to advocate on behalf of the process, and to educate the public. In the mediation, the mediator should encourage effective, nonjudgmental communication between the parties and should model the same. "A mediator shall encourage mutual respect between the parties, and shall take reasonable steps, subject to the principle of self-determination, to limit abuses of the mediation process."[15]

Standard VII: Advertising and Solicitation

Advertising must be honest regarding the mediator's qualifications and not promise successful settlements.

Standard VIII: Fees and Other Charges

If fees are charged, as they are in most private mediations, the amount of the fees and any other charges must be disclosed to the parties at the beginning of the process. It should be determined how the fee responsibility will be divided between the parties.

---

14   SPIDR, Making the Tough Calls, Ethical Exercises for Neutral Dispute Resolvers' 3-4 (1991).

15   Baruch Bush, supra note 10, at 36.

Standard IX: Advancement of Mediation Practice

A mediator is a professional and must behave in such a manner in the promotion of the process and other mediators. Accessibility to the profession and the process is also important. Like all professionals the mediator should engage in continuing education, participate in research when appropriate, and help educate the public. Diverse parties, mediators, and perspectives should be respected.

Arbitration Ethics

There are many ethical codes for arbitrators depending on the area of practice. The Code of Ethics for Arbitrators in Commercial Disputes, developed by the American Arbitration Association and the American Bar Association and dated 2004, is attached hereto as Appendix B. Anyone serving as an arbitrator, or participating in or preparing for arbitration, should be thoroughly familiar with the code of ethics that applies to her area of practice.

Summary

Policy issues relating to ADR include the nature and extent of its integration into the court system. There are arguments on both sides, involving control and resources. A major part of the argument revolves around whether litigants should be required to participate in court-annexed ADR. This is addressed by making mandatory processes nonbinding.

The criticisms of ADR must be evaluated and addressed. They include concern over the privacy of the process, the possibility that ADR may inhibit legal reform, the potential inability to protect weak parties, and the imposition of an additional step in the court process.

The regulation of ADR providers is another policy issue. Current regulation can be found in court connected programs and certification by organizations and states.

The development of any ADR system proceeds on the basis of how well it meets its goals. There should be multiple criteria in measuring the success of any program. In some systems, mediation success is measured by the number of cases settled. This is inappropriate. Mediation offers significant benefits other than settlement, which must be considered in evaluating success.

Regarding policy/ethical issues, there is strong sentiment that some classes of cases should be excluded from ADR or a particular process. Domestic violence and sexual harassment grievances are among those considered for exclusion. Other practitioners, however, maintain it is mistaken to exclude such entire classes of cases.

A neutral requires training in the process in which she is going to practice, e.g., mediation, arbitration, etc. This will familiarize her with the rules and attributes of the process, as well as aid in developing the skills required. Such training, of varying depth, is available from a number of sources. Whether a neutral needs subject matter knowledge (and therefore special training or education) to serve effectively is a more difficult issue. While not required in most cases, such knowledge may be expected by the parties and may help to enrich the neutral's abilities. This varies with the process and the subject matter of the conflict. Theoretical knowledge regarding the process can also enhance the mediator's abilities.

Neutrals are faced with ethical dilemmas on an ongoing basis. Model Standards of Conduct for Mediators, as well as Codes of Ethics for Arbitrators, guide neutrals in this area.

EXERCISES

1. Write a brief paper explaining why ethical standards are essential in any profession.

2. Research your jurisdiction and describe each court-annexed or court-referred ADR program. Determine which processes are used, who serves as neutral, how the program is funded, and how decisions are appealed.

3. Interview a judge, an attorney, and a litigant, each of whom is familiar with or has been through a court-annexed or court-referred ADR process. Determine whether they like or dislike the process and why.

4. Research and discuss five legal issues that went to trial and resulted in new common law being made in the last five years.

5. Determine what the status of regulation or licensure of ADR providers is in your jurisdiction. Is it being discussed or planned?

6. Determine what evaluative processes are being used in your jurisdiction's court-annexed programs.

7. In your jurisdiction, determine which types of cases are excluded from ADR and which groups or constituencies participated in the decision to exclude them and their rationale for their position.

8. Check your state's court rules to determine what training requirements are listed for ADR providers. Is there any subject matter expertise required? Are there higher requirements for custody mediators? Compare your state's training requirements with those of a neighboring state.

9. Find an example of both of the following forms online: Agreement to Mediate and Mediation Agreement.

Model Standards of Conduct for Mediators

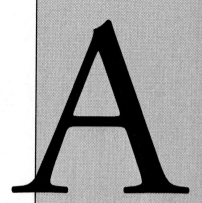

American Arbitration Association
(Adopted September 8, 2005)

American Bar Association
(Adopted August 9, 2005)

Association for Conflict Resolution
(Adopted August 22, 2005)

September 2005

The Model Standards of Conduct for Mediators
September 2005

The *Model Standards of Conduct for Mediators* was prepared in 1994 by the American Arbitration Association, the American Bar Association's Section of Dispute Resolution, and the Association for Conflict Resolution.[1] A joint committee consisting of representatives from the same successor organizations revised the Model Standards in 2005.[2] Both the original 1994 version and the 2005 revision have been approved by each participating organization.[3]

Preamble

Mediation is used to resolve a broad range of conflicts within a variety of settings. These Standards are designed to serve as fundamental ethical guidelines for persons mediating in all practice contexts. They serve three primary goals: to guide the conduct of mediators; to inform the mediating parties; and to promote public confidence in mediation as a process for resolving disputes.

Mediation is a process in which an impartial third party facilitates communication and negotiation and promotes voluntary decision making by the parties to the dispute.

Mediation serves various purposes, including providing the opportunity for parties to define and clarify issues, understand different perspectives, identify interests, explore and assess possible solutions, and reach mutually satisfactory agreements, when desired.

Note on Construction

These Standards are to be read and construed in their entirety. There is no priority significance attached to the sequence in which the Standards appear.

The use of the term "shall" in a Standard indicates that the mediator must follow the practice described. The use of the term "should" indicates that the practice described in the standard is highly desirable, but not required, and is to be departed from only for very strong reasons and requires careful use of judgment and discretion.

---

1   The Association for Conflict Resolution is a merged organization of the Academy of Family Mediators, the Conflict Resolution Education Network and the Society of Professionals in Dispute Resolution (SPIDR). SPIDR was the third participating organization in the development of the 1994 Standards.

2   Reporter's Notes, which are not part of these Standards and therefore have not been specifically approved by any of the organizations, provide commentary regarding these revisions.

3   The 2005 revisions to the Model Standards were approved by the American Bar Association's House of Delegates on August 9, 2005; the Board of the Association for Conflict Resolution on August 22, 2005; and the Executive Committee of the American Arbitration Association on September 8, 2005.

The use of the term "mediator" is understood to be inclusive so that it applies to co-mediator models.

These Standards do not include specific temporal parameters when referencing a mediation and, therefore, do not define the exact beginning or ending of a mediation.

Various aspects of a mediation, including some matters covered by these Standards, may also be affected by applicable law, court rules, regulations, other applicable professional rules, mediation rules to which the parties have agreed and other agreements of the parties. These sources may create conflicts with, and may take precedence over, these Standards. However, a mediator should make every effort to comply with the spirit and intent of these Standards in resolving such conflicts. This effort should include honoring all remaining Standards not in conflict with these other sources.

These Standards, unless and until adopted by a court or other regulatory authority do not have the force of law. Nonetheless, the fact that these Standards have been adopted by the respective sponsoring entities, should alert mediators to the fact that the Standards might be viewed as establishing a standard of care for mediators.

Standard I.   Self-Determination

A.   A mediator shall conduct a mediation based on the principle of party self-determination. Self-determination is the act of coming to a voluntary, uncoerced decision in which each party makes free and informed choices as to process and outcome. Parties may exercise self-determination at any stage of a mediation, including mediator selection, process design, participation in or withdrawal from the process, and outcomes.

> 1.   Although party self-determination for process design is a fundamental principle of mediation practice, a mediator may need to balance such party self-determination with a mediator's duty to conduct a quality process in accordance with these Standards.

> 2.   A mediator cannot personally ensure that each party has made free and informed choices to reach particular decisions, but, where appropriate, a mediator should make the parties aware of the importance of consulting other professionals to help them make informed choices.

B.   A mediator shall not undermine party self-determination by any party for reasons such as higher settlement rates, egos, increased fees, or outside pressures from court personnel, program administrators, provider organizations, the media or others.

Standard II.   Impartiality

A.   A mediator shall decline a mediation if the mediator cannot conduct it in an impartial manner. Impartiality means freedom from favoritism, bias or prejudice.

B.   A mediator shall conduct a mediation in an impartial manner and avoid conduct that gives the appearance of partiality.

1.   A mediator should not act with partiality or prejudice based on any participant's personal characteristics, background, values and beliefs, or performance at a mediation, or any other reason.

2.   A mediator should neither give nor accept a gift, favor, loan or other item of value that raises a question as to the mediator's actual or perceived impartiality.

3.   A mediator may accept or give de minimis gifts or incidental items or services that are provided to facilitate a mediation or respect cultural norms so long as such practices do not raise questions as to a mediator's actual or perceived impartiality,

C.   If at any time a mediator is unable to conduct a mediation in an impartial manner, the mediator shall withdraw.

Standard III.   Conflicts of Interest

A.   A mediator shall avoid a conflict of interest or the appearance of a conflict of interest during and after a mediation. A conflict of interest can arise from involvement by a mediator with the subject matter of the dispute or from any relationship between a mediator and any mediation participant, whether past or present, personal or professional, that reasonably raises a question of a mediator's impartiality.

B.   A mediator shall make a reasonable inquiry to determine whether there are any facts that a reasonable individual would consider likely to create a potential or actual conflict of interest for a mediator. A mediator's actions necessary to accomplish a reasonable inquiry into potential conflicts of interest may vary based on practice context.

C.   A mediator shall disclose, as soon as practicable, all actual and potential conflicts of interest that are reasonably known to the mediator and could reasonably be seen as raising a question about the mediator's impartiality. After disclosure, if all parties agree, the mediator may proceed with the mediation.

D.   If a mediator learns any fact after accepting a mediation that raises a question with respect to that mediator's service creating a potential or actual conflict of interest, the mediator shall disclose it as quickly as practicable. After disclosure, if all parties agree, the mediator may proceed with the mediation.

E.   If a mediator's conflict of interest might reasonably be viewed as undermining the integrity of the mediation, a mediator shall withdraw from or decline to proceed with the mediation regardless of the expressed desire or agreement of the parties to the contrary.

F.   Subsequent to a mediation, a mediator shall not establish another relationship with any of the participants in any matter that would raise questions about the integrity of the mediation. When a mediator develops personal or professional relationships with parties, other individuals or organizations following a mediation in which they were involved, the mediator should consider factors such as time elapsed following the mediation, the nature of the relationships established, and services offered when determining whether the relationships might create a perceived or actual conflict of interest.

Standard IV.   Competence

A.   A mediator shall mediate only when the mediator has the necessary competence to satisfy the reasonable expectations of the parties.

1. Any person may be selected as a mediator, provided that the parties are satisfied with the mediator's competence and qualifications. Training, experience in mediation, skills, cultural understandings and other qualities are often necessary for mediator competence. A person who offers to serve as a mediator creates the expectation that the person is competent to mediate effectively.

2. A mediator should attend educational programs and related activities to maintain and enhance the mediator's knowledge and skills related to mediation.

3. A mediator should have available for the parties' information relevant to the mediator's training, education, experience and approach to conducting a mediation.

B.   If a mediator, during the course of a mediation determines that the mediator cannot conduct the mediation competently, the mediator shall discuss that determination with the parties as soon as is practicable and take appropriate steps to address the situation, including, but not limited to, withdrawing or requesting appropriate assistance.

C.   If a mediator's ability to conduct a mediation is impaired by drugs, alcohol, medication or otherwise, the mediator shall not conduct the mediation.

Standard V.   Confidentiality

A.   A mediator shall maintain the confidentiality of all information obtained by the mediator in mediation, unless otherwise agreed to by the parties or required by applicable law.

> 1.   If the parties to a mediation agree that the mediator may disclose information obtained during the mediation, the mediator may do so.
>
> 2.   A mediator should not communicate to any non-participant information about how the parties acted in the mediation. A mediator may report, if required, whether parties appeared at a scheduled mediation and whether or not the parties reached a resolution.
>
> 3.   If a mediator participates in teaching, research or evaluation of mediation, the mediator should protect the anonymity of the parties and abide by their reasonable expectations regarding confidentiality.

B.   A mediator who meets with any persons in private session during a mediation shall not convey directly or indirectly to any other person, any information that was obtained during that private session without the consent of the disclosing person.

C.   A mediator shall promote understanding among the parties of the extent to which the parties will maintain confidentiality of information they obtain in a mediation.

D.   Depending on the circumstance of a mediation, the parties may have varying expectations regarding confidentiality that a mediator should address. The parties may make their own rules with respect to confidentiality, or the accepted practice of an individual mediator or institution may dictate a particular set of expectations.

Standard VI.   Quality of the Process

A.   A mediator shall conduct a mediation in accordance with these Standards and in a manner that promotes diligence, timeliness, safety, presence of the appropriate participants, party participation, procedural fairness, party competency and mutual respect among all participants.

1. A mediator should agree to mediate only when the mediator is prepared to commit the attention essential to an effective mediation.

2. A mediator should only accept cases when the mediator can satisfy the reasonable expectation of the parties concerning the timing of a mediation.

3. The presence or absence of persons at a mediation depends on the agreement of the parties and the mediator. The parties and mediator may agree that others may be excluded from particular sessions or from all sessions.

4. A mediator should promote honesty and candor between and among all participants, and a mediator shall not knowingly misrepresent any material fact or circumstance in the course of a mediation.

5. The role of a mediator differs substantially from other professional roles. Mixing the role of a mediator and the role of another profession is problematic and thus, a mediator should distinguish between the roles. A mediator may provide information that the mediator is qualified by training or experience to provide, only if the mediator can do so consistent with these Standards.

6. A mediator shall not conduct a dispute resolution procedure other than mediation but label it mediation in an effort to gain the protection of rules, statutes, or other governing authorities pertaining to mediation.

7. A mediator may recommend, when appropriate, that parties consider resolving their dispute through arbitration, counseling, neutral evaluation or other processes.

8. A mediator shall not undertake an additional dispute resolution role in the same matter without the consent of the parties. Before providing such service, a mediator shall inform the parties of the implications of the change in process and obtain their consent to the change. A mediator who undertakes such role assumes different duties and responsibilities that may be governed by other standards.

9. If a mediation is being used to further criminal conduct, a mediator should take appropriate steps including, if necessary, postponing, withdrawing from or terminating the mediation.

10. If a party appears to have difficulty comprehending the process, issues, or settlement options, or difficulty participating in a mediation, the mediator should explore the circumstances and potential accommodations,

modifications or adjustments that would make possible the party's capacity to comprehend, participate and exercise self-determination.

B.   If a mediator is made aware of domestic abuse or violence among the parties, the mediator shall take appropriate steps including, if necessary, postponing, withdrawing from or terminating the mediation.

C.   If a mediator believes that participant conduct, including that of the mediator, jeopardizes conducting a mediation consistent with these Standards, a mediator shall take appropriate steps including, if necessary, postponing, withdrawing from or terminating the mediation.

Standard VII.   Advertising and Solicitation

A.   A mediator shall be truthful and not misleading when advertising, soliciting or otherwise communicating the mediator's qualifications, experience, services and fees.

> 1.   A mediator should not include any promises as to outcome in communications, including business cards, stationery, or computer-based communications.
>
> 2.   A mediator should only claim to meet the mediator qualifications of a governmental entity or private organization if that entity or organization has a recognized procedure for qualifying mediators and it grants such status to the mediator.

B.   A mediator shall not solicit in a manner that gives an appearance of partiality for or against a party or otherwise undermines the integrity of the process.

C.   A mediator shall not communicate to others, in promotional materials or through other forms of communication, the names of persons served without their permission.

Standard VIII.   Fees and Other Charges

A.   A mediator shall provide each party or each party's representative true and complete information about mediation fees, expenses and any other actual or potential charges that may be incurred in connection with a mediation.

> 1.   If a mediator charges fees, the mediator should develop them in light of all relevant factors, including the type and complexity of the matter, the

qualifications of the mediator, the time required and the rates customary for such mediation services.

2. A mediator's fee arrangement should be in writing unless the parties request otherwise.

B. A mediator shall not charge fees in a manner that impairs a mediator's impartiality.

1. A mediator should not enter into a fee agreement which is contingent upon the result of the mediation or amount of the settlement.

2. While a mediator may accept unequal fee payments from the parties, a mediator should not use fee arrangements that adversely impact the mediator's ability to conduct a mediation in an impartial manner.

Standard IX.   Advancement of Mediation Practice

A. A mediator should act in a manner that advances the practice of mediation. A mediator promotes this Standard by engaging in some or all of the following:

1. Fostering diversity within the field of mediation.

2. Striving to make mediation accessible to those who elect to use it, including providing services at a reduced rate or on a pro bono basis as appropriate.

3. Participating in research when given the opportunity, including obtaining participant feedback when appropriate.

4. Participating in outreach and education efforts to assist the public in developing an improved understanding of, and appreciation for, mediation.

5. Assisting newer mediators through training, mentoring and networking.

B. A mediator should demonstrate respect for differing points of view within the field, seek to learn from other mediators and work together with other mediators to improve the profession and better serve people in conflict.

Code of Ethics for Arbitrators in Commercial Disputes

B

Effective March 1, 2004

The Code of Ethics for Arbitrators in Commercial Disputes Effective March 1, 2004

The Code of Ethics for Arbitrators in Commercial Disputes was originally prepared in 1977 by a joint committee consisting of a special committee of the American Arbitration Association and a special committee of the American Bar Association. The Code was revised in 2003 by an ABA Task Force and special committee of the AAA.

Preamble

The use of arbitration to resolve a wide variety of disputes has grown extensively and forms a significant part of the system of justice on which our society relies for a fair determination of legal rights. Persons who act as arbitrators therefore undertake serious responsibilities to the public, as well as to the parties. Those responsibilities include important ethical obligations.

Few cases of unethical behavior by commercial arbitrators have arisen. Nevertheless, this Code sets forth generally accepted standards of ethical conduct for the guidance of arbitrators and parties in commercial disputes, in the hope of contributing to the maintenance of high standards and continued confidence in the process of arbitration.

This Code provides ethical guidelines for many types of arbitration but does not apply to labor arbitration, which is generally conducted under the Code of Professional Responsibility for Arbitrators of Labor-Management Disputes.

There are many different types of commercial arbitration. Some proceedings are conducted under arbitration rules established by various organizations and trade associations, while others are conducted without such rules. Although most proceedings are arbitrated pursuant to voluntary agreement of the parties, certain types of disputes are submitted to arbitration by reason of particular laws. This Code is intended to apply to all such proceedings in which disputes or claims are submitted for decision to one or more arbitrators appointed in a manner provided by an agreement of the parties, by applicable arbitration rules, or by law. In all such cases, the persons who have the power to decide should observe fundamental standards of ethical conduct. In this Code, all such persons are called "arbitrators," although in some types of proceeding they might be called "umpires," "referees," "neutrals," or have some other title.

Arbitrators, like judges, have the power to decide cases. However, unlike full-time judges, arbitrators are usually engaged in other occupations before, during, and after the time that they serve as arbitrators. Often, arbitrators are purposely chosen from the same trade or industry as the parties in order to bring special knowledge to the task of deciding. This Code recognizes these fundamental differences between arbitrators and judges.

In those instances where this Code has been approved and recommended by organizations that provide, coordinate, or administer services of arbitrators, it provides ethical standards for the members of their respective panels of arbitrators. However, this Code does not form a part of the arbitration rules of any such organization unless its rules so provide.

Note on Neutrality

In some types of commercial arbitration, the parties or the administering institution provide for three or more arbitrators. In some such proceedings, it is the practice for each party, acting alone, to appoint one arbitrator (a "party-appointed arbitrator") and for one additional arbitrator to be designated by the party-appointed arbitrators, or by the parties, or by an independent institution or individual. The sponsors of this Code believe that it is preferable for all arbitrators including any party-appointed arbitrators to be neutral, that is, independent and impartial, and to comply with the same ethical standards. This expectation generally is essential in arbitrations where the parties, the nature of the dispute, or the enforcement of any resulting award may have international aspects. However, parties in certain domestic arbitrations in the United States may prefer that party-appointed arbitrators be non-neutral and governed by special ethical considerations. These special ethical considerations appear in Canon X of this Code.

This Code establishes a presumption of neutrality for all arbitrators, including party-appointed arbitrators, which applies unless the parties' agreement, the arbitration rules agreed to by the parties or applicable laws provide otherwise. This Code requires all party-appointed arbitrators, whether neutral or not, to make pre-appointment disclosures of any facts which might affect their neutrality, independence, or impartiality. This Code also requires all party-appointed arbitrators to ascertain and disclose as soon as practicable whether the parties intended for them to serve as neutral or not. If any doubt or uncertainty exists, the party-appointed arbitrators should serve as neutrals unless and until such doubt or uncertainty is resolved in accordance with Canon IX. This Code expects all arbitrators, including those serving under Canon X, to preserve the integrity and fairness of the process.

Note on Construction

Various aspects of the conduct of arbitrators, including some matters covered by this Code, may also be governed by agreements of the parties, arbitration rules to which the parties have agreed, applicable law, or other applicable ethics rules, all of which should be consulted by the arbitrators. This Code does not take the place of or supersede such laws, agreements, or arbitration rules to which the parties have agreed and should be read in conjunction with other rules of ethics. It does not establish new or additional grounds for judicial review of arbitration awards.

All provisions of this Code should therefore be read as subject to contrary provisions of applicable law and arbitration rules. They should also be read as subject to contrary agreements of the parties. Nevertheless, this Code imposes no obligation on any arbitrator to act in a manner inconsistent with the arbitrator's fundamental duty to preserve the integrity and fairness of the arbitral process.

Canons I through VIII of this Code apply to all arbitrators. Canon IX applies to all party-appointed arbitrators, except that certain party-appointed arbitrators are exempted by Canon X from compliance with certain provisions of Canons I-IX related to impartiality and independence, as specified in Canon X.

Canon I: An Arbitrator Should Uphold the Integrity and Fairness of the Arbitration Process

A.   An arbitrator has a responsibility not only to the parties but also to the process of arbitration itself, and must observe high standards of conduct so that the integrity and fairness of the process will be preserved. Accordingly, an arbitrator should recognize a responsibility to the public, to the parties whose rights will be decided, and to all other participants in the proceeding. This responsibility may include pro bono service as an arbitrator where appropriate.

B.   One should accept appointment as an arbitrator only if fully satisfied:

(1)   that he or she can serve impartially;

(2)   that he or she can serve independently from the parties, potential witnesses, and the other arbitrators;

(3)   that he or she is competent to serve; and

(4)   that he or she can be available to commence the arbitration in accordance with the requirements of the proceeding and thereafter to devote the time and attention to its completion that the parties are reasonably entitled to expect.

C.   After accepting appointment and while serving as an arbitrator, a person should avoid entering into any business, professional, or personal relationship, or acquiring any financial or personal interest, which is likely to affect impartiality or which might reasonably create the appearance of partiality. For a reasonable period of time after the decision of a case, persons who have served as arbitrators should avoid entering into any such relationship, or acquiring any such interest, in circumstances which might reasonably create the appearance that they had been influenced in the arbitration by the anticipation or expectation of the relationship or interest. Existence of any of the matters or circumstances described in this paragraph C does not render it unethical for one to serve as an arbitrator where the parties have consented to the arbitrator's appointment or continued services following full disclosure of the relevant facts in accordance with Canon II.

D.   Arbitrators should conduct themselves in a way that is fair to all parties and should not be swayed by outside pressure, public clamor, and fear of criticism or self-interest. They should avoid conduct and statements that give the appearance of partiality toward or against any party.

E.   When an arbitrator's authority is derived from the agreement of the parties, an arbitrator should neither exceed that authority nor do less than is required to exercise that authority completely. Where the agreement of the parties sets forth procedures to be followed in conducting the arbitration or refers to rules to be followed, it is the obligation of the arbitrator to comply with such procedures or rules. An arbitrator has no ethical obligation to comply with any agreement, procedures or rules that are unlawful or that, in the arbitrator's judgment, would be inconsistent with this Code.

F.   An arbitrator should conduct the arbitration process so as to advance the fair and efficient resolution of the matters submitted for decision. An arbitrator should make all reasonable efforts to prevent delaying tactics, harassment of parties or other participants, or other abuse or disruption of the arbitration process.

G.   The ethical obligations of an arbitrator begin upon acceptance of the appointment and continue throughout all stages of the proceeding. In addition, as set forth in this Code, certain ethical obligations begin as soon as a person is requested to serve as an arbitrator and certain ethical obligations continue after the decision in the proceeding has been given to the parties.

H.   Once an arbitrator has accepted an appointment, the arbitrator should not withdraw or abandon the appointment unless compelled to do so by unanticipated circumstances that would render it impossible or impracticable to continue. When an arbitrator is to be compensated for his or her services, the arbitrator may withdraw if the parties fail or refuse to provide for payment of the compensation as agreed.

I.   An arbitrator who withdraws prior to the completion of the arbitration, whether upon the arbitrator's initiative or upon the request of one or more of the parties, should take reasonable steps to protect the interests of the parties in the arbitration, including return of evidentiary materials and protection of confidentiality.

Comment to Canon I

A prospective arbitrator is not necessarily partial or prejudiced by having acquired knowledge of the parties, the applicable law or the customs and practices of the business involved. Arbitrators may also have special experience or expertise in the areas of business, commerce, or technology which are involved in the arbitration. Arbitrators do not contravene this Canon if, by virtue of such experience or expertise, they have views on certain general issues likely to arise in the arbitration, but an arbitrator may not have prejudged any of the specific factual or legal determinations to be addressed during the arbitration.

During an arbitration, the arbitrator may engage in discourse with the parties or their counsel, draw out arguments or contentions, comment on the law or evidence, make interim rulings, and otherwise control or direct the arbitration. These activities are integral parts of an arbitration. Paragraph D of Canon I is not intended to preclude or limit either full discussion of the issues during the course of the arbitration or the arbitrator's management of the proceeding.

Canon II: An Arbitrator Should Disclose Any Interest or Relationship Likely to Affect Impartiality or Which Might Create an Appearance of Partiality

A.   Persons who are requested to serve as arbitrators should, before accepting, disclose:

(1)   any known direct or indirect financial or personal interest in the outcome of the arbitration;

(2)   any known existing or past financial, business, professional or personal relationships which might reasonably affect impartiality or lack of independence in the eyes of any of the parties. For example, prospective arbitrators should disclose any such relationships which they personally

have with any party or its lawyer, with any co-arbitrator, or with any individual whom they have been told will be a witness. They should also disclose any such relationships involving their families or household members or their current employers, partners, or professional or business associates that can be ascertained by reasonable efforts;

(3)   the nature and extent of any prior knowledge they may have of the dispute; and

(4)   any other matters, relationships, or interests which they are obligated to disclose by the agreement of the parties, the rules or practices of an institution, or applicable law regulating arbitrator disclosure.

B.   Persons who are requested to accept appointment as arbitrators should make a reasonable effort to inform themselves of any interests or relationships described in paragraph A.

C.   The obligation to disclose interests or relationships described in paragraph A is a continuing duty which requires a person who accepts appointment as an arbitrator to disclose, as soon as practicable, at any stage of the arbitration, any such interests or relationships which may arise, or which are recalled or discovered.

D.   Any doubt as to whether or not disclosure is to be made should be resolved in favor of disclosure.

E.   Disclosure should be made to all parties unless other procedures for disclosure are provided in the agreement of the parties, applicable rules or practices of an institution, or by law. Where more than one arbitrator has been appointed, each should inform the others of all matters disclosed.

F.   When parties, with knowledge of a person's interests and relationships, nevertheless desire that person to serve as an arbitrator, that person may properly serve.

G.   If an arbitrator is requested by all parties to withdraw, the arbitrator must do so. If an arbitrator is requested to withdraw by less than all of the parties because of alleged partiality, the arbitrator should withdraw unless either of the following circumstances exists:

(1)   An agreement of the parties, or arbitration rules agreed to by the parties, or applicable law establishes procedures for determining challenges to arbitrators, in which case those procedures should be followed; or

(2)   In the absence of applicable procedures, if the arbitrator, after carefully considering the matter, determines that the reason for the challenge is not

substantial, and that he or she can nevertheless act and decide the case impartially and fairly.

H.   If compliance by a prospective arbitrator with any provision of this Code would require disclosure of confidential or privileged information, the prospective arbitrator should either:

(1)   Secure the consent to the disclosure from the person who furnished the information or the holder of the privilege; or

(2)   Withdraw.

Canon III: An Arbitrator Should Avoid Impropriety or the Appearance of Impropriety in Communicating with Parties

A.   If an agreement of the parties or applicable arbitration rules establishes the manner or content of communications between the arbitrator and the parties, the arbitrator should follow those procedures notwithstanding any contrary provision of paragraphs B and C.

B.   An arbitrator or prospective arbitrator should not discuss a proceeding with any party in the absence of any other party, except in any of the following circumstances:

(1) When the appointment of a prospective arbitrator is being considered, the prospective arbitrator:

(a)   may ask about the identities of the parties, counsel, or witnesses and the general nature of the case; and

(b)   may respond to inquiries from a party or its counsel designed to determine his or her suitability and availability for the appointment. In any such dialogue, the prospective arbitrator may receive information from a party or its counsel disclosing the general nature of the dispute but should not permit them to discuss the merits of the case.

(2) In an arbitration in which the two party-appointed arbitrators are expected to appoint the third arbitrator, each party-appointed arbitrator may consult with the party who appointed the arbitrator concerning the choice of the third arbitrator;

(3) In an arbitration involving party-appointed arbitrators, each party-appointed arbitrator may consult with the party who appointed the arbitrator concerning arrangements for any compensation to be paid to the party-appointed arbitrator. Submission of routine written requests for payment of compensation and expenses in accordance with such arrangements and written communications pertaining solely to such requests need not be sent to the other party;

(4) In an arbitration involving party-appointed arbitrators, each party-appointed arbitrator may consult with the party who appointed the arbitrator concerning the status of the arbitrator (*i.e.*, neutral or non-neutral), as contemplated by paragraph C of Canon IX;

(5) Discussions may be had with a party concerning such logistical matters as setting the time and place of hearings or making other arrangements for the conduct of the proceedings. However, the arbitrator should promptly inform each other party of the discussion and should not make any final determination concerning the matter discussed before giving each absent party an opportunity to express the party's views; or

(6) If a party fails to be present at a hearing after having been given due notice, or if all parties expressly consent, the arbitrator may discuss the case with any party who is present.

C.   Unless otherwise provided in this Canon, in applicable arbitration rules or in an agreement of the parties, whenever an arbitrator communicates in writing with one party, the arbitrator should at the same time send a copy of the communication to every other party, and whenever the arbitrator receives any written communication concerning the case from one party which has not already been sent to every other party, the arbitrator should send or cause it to be sent to the other parties.

Canon IV: An Arbitrator Should Conduct the Proceedings Fairly and Diligently

A.   An arbitrator should conduct the proceedings in an even-handed manner. The arbitrator should be patient and courteous to the parties, their representatives, and the witnesses and should encourage similar conduct by all participants.

B.   The arbitrator should afford to all parties the right to be heard and due notice of the time and place of any hearing. The arbitrator should allow each party a fair opportunity to present its evidence and arguments.

C.   The arbitrator should not deny any party the opportunity to be represented by counsel or by any other person chosen by the party.

D.   If a party fails to appear after due notice, the arbitrator should proceed with the arbitration when authorized to do so, but only after receiving assurance that appropriate notice has been given to the absent party.

E.   When the arbitrator determines that more information than has been presented by the parties is required to decide the case, it is not improper for the arbitrator to ask questions, call witnesses, and request documents or other evidence, including expert testimony.

F.   Although it is not improper for an arbitrator to suggest to the parties that they discuss the possibility of settlement or the use of mediation, or other dispute resolution processes, an arbitrator should not exert pressure on any party to settle or to utilize other dispute resolution processes. An arbitrator should not be present or otherwise participate in settlement discussions or act as a mediator unless requested to do so by all parties.

G.   Co-arbitrators should afford each other full opportunity to participate in all aspects of the proceedings.

Comment to Paragraph G

Paragraph G of Canon IV is not intended to preclude one arbitrator from acting in limited circumstances (e.g., ruling on discovery issues) where authorized by the agreement of the parties, applicable rules or law, nor does it preclude a majority of the arbitrators from proceeding with any aspect of the arbitration if an arbitrator is unable or unwilling to participate and such action is authorized by the agreement of the parties or applicable rules or law. It also does not preclude ex parte requests for interim relief.

Canon V: An Arbitrator Should Make Decisions in a Just, Independent and Deliberate Manner

A.   The arbitrator should, after careful deliberation, decide all issues submitted for determination. An arbitrator should decide no other issues.

B.   An arbitrator should decide all matters justly, exercising independent judgment, and should not permit outside pressure to affect the decision.

C.   An arbitrator should not delegate the duty to decide to any other person.

D.   In the event that all parties agree upon a settlement of issues in dispute and request the arbitrator to embody that agreement in an award, the arbitrator may do so, but is not required to do so unless satisfied with the propriety of the terms of settlement. Whenever an arbitrator embodies a settlement by the parties in an award, the arbitrator should state in the award that it is based on an agreement of the parties.

Canon VI: An Arbitrator Should Be Faithful to the Relationship of Trust and Confidentiality Inherent in That Office

A.   An arbitrator is in a relationship of trust to the parties and should not, at any time, use confidential information acquired during the arbitration proceeding to gain personal advantage or advantage for others, or to affect adversely the interest of another.

B.   The arbitrator should keep confidential all matters relating to the arbitration proceedings and decision. An arbitrator may obtain help from an associate, a research assistant or other persons in connection with reaching his or her decision if the arbitrator informs the parties of the use of such assistance and such persons agree to be bound by the provisions of this Canon.

C.   It is not proper at any time for an arbitrator to inform anyone of any decision in advance of the time it is given to all parties. In a proceeding in which there is more than one arbitrator, it is not proper at any time for an arbitrator to inform anyone about the substance of the deliberations of the arbitrators. After an arbitration award has been made, it is not proper for an arbitrator to assist in proceedings to enforce or challenge the award.

D.   Unless the parties so request, an arbitrator should not appoint himself or herself to a separate office related to the subject matter of the dispute, such as receiver or trustee, nor should a panel of arbitrators appoint one of their number to such an office.

Canon VII: An Arbitrator Should Adhere to Standards of Integrity and Fairness When Making Arrangements for Compensation and Reimbursement of Expenses

A.   Arbitrators who are to be compensated for their services or reimbursed for their expenses shall adhere to standards of integrity and fairness in making arrangements for such payments.

B.   Certain practices relating to payments are generally recognized as tending to preserve the integrity and fairness of the arbitration process. These practices include:

(1)   Before the arbitrator finally accepts appointment, the basis of payment, including any cancellation fee, compensation in the event of withdrawal and compensation for study and preparation time, and all other charges, should be established. Except for arrangements for the compensation of party-appointed arbitrators, all parties should be informed in writing of the terms established;

(2)   In proceedings conducted under the rules or administration of an institution that is available to assist in making arrangements for payments, communication related to compensation should be made through the institution. In proceedings where no institution has been engaged by the parties to administer the arbitration, any communication with arbitrators (other than party-appointed arbitrators) concerning payments should be in the presence of all parties; and

(3)   Arbitrators should not, absent extraordinary circumstances, request increases in the basis of their compensation during the course of a proceeding.

Canon VIII: An Arbitrator May Engage in Advertising or Promotion of Arbitral Services Which Is Truthful and Accurate

A.   Advertising or promotion of an individual's willingness or availability to serve as an arbitrator must be accurate and unlikely to mislead. Any statements about the quality of the arbitrator's work or the success of the arbitrator's practice must be truthful.

B.   Advertising and promotion must not imply any willingness to accept an appointment otherwise than in accordance with this Code.

Comment to Canon VIII

This Canon does not preclude an arbitrator from printing, publishing, or disseminating advertisements conforming to these standards in any electronic or print medium, from making personal presentations to prospective users of arbitral services conforming to such standards or from responding to inquiries concerning the arbitrator's availability, qualifications, experience, or fee arrangements.

Canon IX: Arbitrators Appointed by One Party Have a Duty to Determine and Disclose Their Status and to Comply with This Code, Except as Exempted by Canon X

A.   In some types of arbitration in which there are three arbitrators, it is customary for each party, acting alone, to appoint one arbitrator. The third arbitrator is then appointed by agreement either of the parties or of the two arbitrators, or failing such agreement, by an independent institution or individual. In tripartite arbitrations to which this Code applies, all three arbitrators are presumed to be neutral and are expected to observe the same standards as the third arbitrator.

B.   Notwithstanding this presumption, there are certain types of tripartite arbitration in which it is expected by all parties that the two arbitrators appointed by the parties may be predisposed toward the party appointing them. Those arbitrators, referred to in this Code as "Canon X arbitrators," are not to be held to the standards of neutrality and independence applicable to other arbitrators. Canon X describes the special ethical obligations of party-appointed arbitrators who are not expected to meet the standard of neutrality.

C.   A party-appointed arbitrator has an obligation to ascertain, as early as possible but not later than the first meeting of the arbitrators and parties, whether the parties have agreed that the party-appointed arbitrators will serve as neutrals or whether they shall be subject to Canon X, and to provide a timely report of their conclusions to the parties and other arbitrators:

> (1)   Party-appointed arbitrators should review the agreement of the parties, the applicable rules and any applicable law bearing upon arbitrator neutrality. In reviewing the agreement of the parties, party-appointed arbitrators should consult any relevant express terms of the written or oral arbitration agreement. It may also be appropriate for them to inquire into agreements that have not been expressly set forth, but which may be implied from an established course of dealings of the parties or well-recognized custom and usage in their trade or profession;

> (2)   Where party-appointed arbitrators conclude that the parties intended for the party-appointed arbitrators are not to serve as neutrals, they should so inform the parties and the other arbitrators. The arbitrators may then act as provided in Canon X unless or until a different determination of their

status is made by the parties, any administering institution or the arbitral panel; and

(3) Until party-appointed arbitrators conclude that the party-appointed arbitrators were not intended by the parties to serve as neutrals, or if the party-appointed arbitrators are unable to form a reasonable belief of their status from the foregoing sources and no decision in this regard has yet been made by the parties, any administering institution, or the arbitral panel, they should observe all of the obligations of neutral arbitrators set forth in this Code.

D.   Party-appointed arbitrators not governed by Canon X shall observe all of the obligations of Canons I through VIII unless otherwise required by agreement of the parties, any applicable rules, or applicable law.

Canon X: Exemptions for Arbitrators Appointed by One Party Who Are Not Subject to Rules of Neutrality

Canon X arbitrators are expected to observe all of the ethical obligations prescribed by this Code except those from which they are specifically excused by Canon X.

A. Obligations under Canon I

Canon X arbitrators should observe all of the obligations of Canon I subject only to the following provisions:

(1)   Canon X arbitrators may be predisposed toward the party who appointed them but in all other respects are obligated to act in good faith and with integrity and fairness. For example, Canon X arbitrators should not engage in delaying tactics or harassment of any party or witness and should not knowingly make untrue or misleading statements to the other arbitrators; and

(2)   The provisions of subparagraphs B(1), B(2), and paragraphs C and D of Canon I, insofar as they relate to partiality, relationships, and interests are not applicable to Canon X arbitrators.

B. Obligations under Canon II

(1)   Canon X arbitrators should disclose to all parties, and to the other arbitrators, all interests and relationships which Canon II requires be disclosed. Disclosure as

required by Canon II is for the benefit not only of the party who appointed the arbitrator, but also for the benefit of the other parties and arbitrators so that they may know of any partiality which may exist or appear to exist; and

(2)   Canon X arbitrators are not obliged to withdraw under paragraph G of Canon II if requested to do so only by the party who did not appoint them.

C. Obligations under Canon III

Canon X arbitrators should observe all of the obligations of Canon III subject only to the following provisions:

(1)   Like neutral party-appointed arbitrators, Canon X arbitrators may consult with the party who appointed them to the extent permitted in paragraph B of Canon III;

(2)   Canon X arbitrators shall, at the earliest practicable time, disclose to the other arbitrators and to the parties whether or not they intend to communicate with their appointing parties. If they have disclosed the intention to engage in such communications, they may thereafter communicate with their appointing parties concerning any other aspect of the case, except as provided in paragraph (3);

(3)   If such communication occurred prior to the time they were appointed as arbitrators, or prior to the first hearing or other meeting of the parties with the arbitrators, the Canon X arbitrator should, at or before the first hearing or meeting of the arbitrators with the parties, disclose the fact that such communication has taken place. In complying with the provisions of this subparagraph, it is sufficient that there be disclosure of the fact that such communication has occurred without disclosing the content of the communication. A single timely disclosure of the Canon X arbitrator's intention to participate in such communications in the future is sufficient;

(4)   Canon X arbitrators may not at any time during the arbitration:

   (a)   disclose any deliberations by the arbitrators on any matter or issue submitted to them for decision;

   (b)   communicate with the parties that appointed them concerning any matter or issue taken under consideration by the panel after the record is closed or such matter or issue has been submitted for decision; or

   (c)   disclose any final decision or interim decision in advance of the time that it is disclosed to all parties.

(5)   Unless otherwise agreed by the arbitrators and the parties, a Canon X arbitrator may not communicate orally with the neutral arbitrator concerning any matter or issue arising or expected to arise in the arbitration in the absence of the other Canon X arbitrator. If a Canon X arbitrator communicates in writing with the neutral arbitrator, he or she shall simultaneously provide a copy of the written communication to the other Canon X arbitrator;

(6)   When Canon X arbitrators communicate orally with the parties that appointed them concerning any matter on which communication is permitted under this Code, they are not obligated to disclose the contents of such oral communications to any other party or arbitrator; and

(7)   When Canon X arbitrators communicate in writing with the party who appointed them concerning any matter on which communication is permitted under this Code, they are not required to send copies of any such written communication to any other party or arbitrator.

D. Obligations under Canon IV

Canon X arbitrators should observe all of the obligations of Canon IV.

E. Obligations under Canon V

Canon X arbitrators should observe all of the obligations of Canon V, except that they may be predisposed toward deciding in favor of the party who appointed them.

F. Obligations under Canon VI

Canon X arbitrators should observe all of the obligations of Canon VI.

G. Obligations under Canon VII

Canon X arbitrators should observe all of the obligations of Canon VII.

H. Obligations under Canon VIII

Canon X arbitrators should observe all of the obligations of Canon VIII.

I. Obligations under Canon IX

The provisions of paragraph D of Canon IX are inapplicable to Canon X arbitrators, except insofar as the obligations are also set forth in this Canon.

Example of Med-Arb*

---

* Taken from Susan M. Leeson & Bryan M. Johnston, Ending It: Dispute Resolution in America 151-153 (1988).

John Cotesworth, Evan Handy, and Cynthia Paul attended veterinary school together in the mid-1960s. During school they were best friends and decided to go into partnership together in a small town in the mid-west when they graduated. Because they were such close friends they decided to run their practice on a very informal basis. They each contributed money to buy equipment and supplies, rent a clinic, and advertise their services. Handy's father had been a veterinarian and gave them a lot of good advice, some equipment, and his patient list when he retired. Cotesworth, Handy, and Paul agreed to share profits equally.

For almost 15 years the practice went quite smoothly. The clinic developed an excellent reputation in the community and each of the veterinarians was highly respected and well known. Paul served three terms as mayor, Cotesworth was active in United Way, and Handy was named Citizen of the Year in 1984 for his work with senior citizens.

In May 1986, the three started to have problems. Cotesworth and his wife were divorced after several months of a child custody battle. Cotesworth's ex-wife remained Cynthia Paul's best friend, and Paul found it increasingly hard to work with Cotesworth given what his former wife told her about him. Handy, who had always been a social drinker, began occasionally to show up for work intoxicated or hung over and sometimes was unable to perform even routine surgeries. Cotesworth had no patience with Handy's drinking and would refuse to speak to Handy for several days.

Soon these personal problems started having professional ramifications. Cotesworth felt that because he was single, Paul and Handy expected him to do most of the weekend emergency work but were unwilling to compensate him for it. Paul felt that both Cotesworth and Handy assigned the particularly sensitive cases to her because of her diplomacy with people and her ability to calm nervous animals. By mid-year the three veterinarians could barely speak to one another and realized that they should stop trying to work together.

Every time Cotesworth, Handy, and Paul tried to discuss the best way to end their partnership they got into serious arguments. None was content with a three-way split. Paul and Cotesworth felt they had contributed much more than their share of time to the practice, while Handy contended they should not be allowed to benefit from all the help they had received from his father when they were starting their practice. Neither Cotesworth nor Paul wanted to stop practicing veterinary medicine, although Handy readily admitted that he was ready for a career change. Both Cotesworth and Paul wanted the equipment and the clinic; Handy said he would rather sell his share to anybody else than Cotesworth and Paul.

Cotesworth finally consulted his lawyer about the best way to dissolve the partnership. His attorney asked to see a copy of the original partnership agreement in order to study the provisions for dissolution. Cotesworth explained that when the three had started out they were best friends and that they had operated all these years without a partnership agreement. Cotesworth's lawyer listened to her client's explanation of the problem confronting the veterinarians and explained med-arb. The three could try to negotiate a settlement to their dispute with the aid of a neutral mediator. Lacking agreement, the mediator either could offer an opinion or could turn the dispute over to an arbitrator. Cotesworth's lawyer gave him a list of three people in the community who practice mediation.

Cotesworth, Handy and Paul interviewed the three mediators and agreed that one would be acceptable. They also agreed that they did not want everyone in the town to know about their problems and concluded that the mediator should be authorized to arbitrate the dispute if they were unable to resolve their dispute. When they met, the mediator spent several hours with the three explaining mediation and establishing ground rules. Achieving agreement on a process was a big step. In addition to agreeing on a process, they agreed to meet twice a week for two hours until they either came to agreement or reached stalemate.

The three veterinarians stayed in mediation for almost five weeks. Sometimes they met together, sometimes the mediator met with them individually or in pairs. The mediator was able to get them to talk about what had happened to their friendship as well as the best way to dissolve the partnership. Cotesworth finally understood that Paul had been angry with him because of his divorce and comments from his ex-wife. He had thought she disapproved of the way he had handled a case several months ago and was holding a grudge. Cotesworth and Paul both came to a better understanding of Handy's drinking problem, apparently precipitated by the fact that he no longer liked veterinary medicine but thought he was too old to make a career change. Cotesworth and Handy listened to Paul's resentment about being given the most difficult patients. All were able to acknowledge how important their friendship had been over the years.

Through mediation Cotesworth and Paul were able to agree that they both wanted to continue to practice veterinary medicine in the same town and that they did not want to be in competition with one another. They knew, however, that they would never be close friends as they once had been. They agreed to retain a lawyer to draw up a formal partnership agreement.

Despite their progress in mediation, the three were not able to agree how much Handy should be paid for his share of the partnership. That issue eventually was turned over to the mediator, now arbitrator, for a decision. Cotesworth and Paul then agreed on what percentage of the award each of them should pay Handy. Handy used his share of the settlement to relocate in another community to work with a group of cattle breeders.

Bibliography

American Arbitration Association & American Bar Association, Code of Ethics for Arbitrators in Commercial Disputes (2004).

American Arbitration Association, American Bar Association & Association for Conflict Resolution, Model Standards of Conduct for Mediators (2005).

American Bar Association, Model Rules of Professional Conduct 4.1(a), 4.2(a) (2002).

American Heritage Dictionary of the English Language (4th ed. 2000)

Black's Law Dictionary (8th ed. 2004).

Breslin, J. William & Rubin, Jeffrey Z., eds., Negotiation Theory and Practice. (1991)

Bush, Robert A. Baruch, The Dilemmas of Mediation Practice: A Study of Ethical Dilemmas and Policy Implications (National Institute for Dispute Resolution) (1992).

Bush, Robert A. Baruch & Folger, Joseph P., The Promise of Mediation (2005).

Chasen, Andrea Nager, Defining Mediation and Its Use for Paralegals, 9 J. Paralegal Educ. Prac. 64 (April 1993).

Chernick, Richard, Private Judging, 3 BNA Alternative Disp. Resol. Rep. 397 (1989).

Coulson, Robert, How to Stay Out of Court (1985).

Domenici, Kathy, Mediation: Empowerment in Conflict Management (1996).

Federal Rules of Civil Procedure 68.

Firestone, Gregory, Court ADR Systems: The Road Ahead, ACResolution (2007).

Fisher, Roger, & Ury, William, Getting to Yes (2d ed. 1991).

Folberg, Jay & Taylor, Alison, Mediation: A Comprehensive Guide to Resolving Conflicts Without Litigation (1984).

Forlenza, Samuel G., Mediation and Psychotherapy: Parallel Processes, Community Mediation: A Handbook for Practitioners and Researchers (Karen Grover Duffy, James W. Grosch & Paul V. Olczak, eds., 1991).

Forum, National Institute for Dispute Resolution 11.3 (1994).

Forum, National Institute for Dispute Resolution, No. 26 (Summer 1994).

Gale, Dick S., ADR at the Crossroads, Disp. Resol. J. (March 1994).

Goldberg, Stephen B., Sander, Frank E. A. & Rogers, Nancy H., Dispute Resolution: Negotiation, Mediation, and Other Processes (5th ed. 2007).

Irvine, Mori, Mediation: Is it Appropriate for Sexual Harassment Grievances?, 9 Ohio St. J. Disp. Resol. 28 (1993).

Kerr, Charles A., In Mediation What Am I?, The Alternative, Dispute Resolution Center of Snohomish and Island Counties, Everett, Washington (Spring 1993).

Kovach, Kimberlee K., Mediation, Principles, and Practice (3rd ed. 2004).

Kruger, Judith A. & Duryea, Michelle LeBaron, The Tapestry of Culture: A Design for the Assessment of Intercultural Disputes, at 68, *in* Taking Stock, 1992 Proceedings of 20th Annual Conference of Society of Professionals in Dispute Resolution, Oct. 1992, Washington.

Lambros, Thomas, Summary Jury Trial — An Alternative Method of Resolving Disputes, 69 Judicature 286 (1986).

Leeson, Susan M. & Johnston, Bryan M., Ending It: Dispute Resolution in America (1988).

Lerman, Lisa G., Mediation of Wife Abuse Cases: The Adverse Impact of Informal Dispute Resolution on Women, 7 Harv. Women's L.J. 57, 72 (1984).

Mandated Participation and Settlement Coercion: Dispute Resolution as it Relates to the Courts, Report #1 of the Law and Public Policy Committee (1991), Society of Professionals in Dispute Resolution, Washington.

Maselko, C. James, Support/Confrontation (1980).

_____,The Fair Fight (Effective Aggression) (1985).

McEwen, Craig & Maiman, Richard J., Small Claims Mediation in Maine: An Empirical Assessment, *in* Stephen B. Goldberg et al., Dispute Resolution: Negotiation, Mediation, and Other Processes 148-155 (5th ed. 2007).

McIver, John P. & Keilitz, Susan, Court-Annexed Arbitration: An Introduction, 13 Justice Sys. J. 123 (1991).

Moore, Christopher W., The Mediation Process (3d ed. 2003).

Myers, Selma & Filner, Barbara, Mediation Across Cultures: A Handbook about Conflict & Culture (1994).

National Association for Legal Assistants Canons (2004).

Nemeth, Charles P., Litigation, Pleadings and Arbitration (1990).

Oxford English Dictionary (2d ed. 2005).

Peppet, Scott R., Rau, Alan Scott & Sherman, Edward F., Process of Dispute Resolution: The Role of Lawyers (4th ed. 2006).

Raiffa, Howard, The Art & Science of Negotiation (1982). (Reprinted 2005).

Rowe, Mary P., The Corporate Ombudsman: An Overview and Analysis, *in* Negotiation Theory and Practice 433-434 (J. William Breslin & Jeffrey Z. Rubin eds. 1993).

Sander, Frank E. A., The Courthouse and Alternative Dispute Resolution, *reprinted in* Negotiation Strategies for Mutual Gain: The Basic Seminar of the Program on Negotiation at Harvard Law School (1993).

Scott, Gini Graham, Disagreements, Disputes, and All Out War (2007).

Singer, Linda R., Settling Disputes: Conflict Resolution in Business, Families, and the Legal System (2d ed. 1994).

Society for Professionals in Dispute Resolution, Making the Tough Calls: Exercises for Neutral Dispute Resolvers (1991).

Tractenberg, Paul L., New Jersey Dispute Resolution: A Lawyer's Guide to State and Federal Court Programs (1994).

Worchel, Stephen & Simpson, Jeffrey A., eds., Conflict Between People and Groups (1993).

Yarn, Douglas H., ed., Dictionary of Conflict Resolution (1999).

Zartman, I. William & Towal, Saadia, International Mediation *in* Leashing the Dogs of War (Chester A. Crocker et. al., eds., 2007).

Index